Sport Psychology

An A Level Guide for Teachers and Students

Simon Webster

Jan Roscoe Publications

Published by :
Jan Roscoe Publications
Holyrood 23 Stockswell Road
Widnes
Cheshire WA8 4PJ
UK

tel - 0151 420 4446
fax - 0151 495 2622
E-mail - jroscoe@rapid.co.uk
Internet - http://www.jroscoe.co.uk

ISBN : 1 901424 09 X

INTRODUCTION

This book consists of a collection of notes and explanations suitable for background information for teachers of A level Physical Education or Sport Studies , or as student notes for those at the receiving end of the same courses.

At the time of going to press , there are two syllabuses available at A level :

AEB (Associated Examining Board) Physical Education or Sport Studies . This is a single core syllabus incorporating Skill Acquisition and Sport Psychology , which branches into Physical Education or Sport Studies depending on whether practical or project based options are chosen.

OCEAC (Oxford and Cambridge Examinations and Assessment Council) Physical Education . This syllabus includes Skill Acquisition as part of the core , and Sport Psychology as an optional block of study (normally to be studied in the second year of the course).

The work from which the book has evolved has depended on about seven years of A level teaching - thereby finding the best use of words and examples to illustrate points of theory.

Pages from the book are photocopy free within the purchasing institution , and should provide a complete and concise set of notes for the aspiring A level learner .

Dennis Roscoe (Editor)

Sport Psychology - An A level Guide for Teachers and Students
Section 1 - Acquisition of Skill

Chapter 6 - Information Processing

Chapter 7 - Stages of Learning

Sport Psychology - An A level Guide for Teachers and Students

Section 1 - Acquisition of Skill

Chapter 1 - Ability

The Characteristics of Skills and Abilities which are Motor and Perceptual
Definitions
Types of Ability
The Concept of the Natural All-round Athlete

Chapter 1 - Ability

THE CHARACTERISTICS OF SKILLS AND ABILITIES WHICH ARE MOTOR AND PERCEPTUAL

DEFINITIONS

Skill :   The learned capacity to bring about a predetermined result using the minimum of time or effort or both.
Skill is the capacity to make the difficult seem easy.

Ability :   A general capacity of an individual. Ability is inherited. A skill is learned.

TYPES OF ABILITY

Fleishman was one of the first to identify the existence of different perceptual motor abilities. The actual number of different perceptual motor abilities is difficult to predict, and the number may be more than fifty.

Major perceptual motor abilities include :

- ❏ **co-ordination**
- ❏ **speed**
- ❏ **reaction time**
- ❏ **balance**
- ❏ **agility**
- ❏ **manual dexterity**
- ❏ **depth perception**

Ability is different from skill. According to **Schmidt** :

ABILITY	SKILL
inherited	learned and developed with practice
stable and enduring	modified with practice
perhaps more than 50	infinite in number
underlie many skills	depends on several abilities

Skill is the **application** of **ability**.
Skills are **learned** using existing abilities.

THE CONCEPT OF THE NATURAL ALL-ROUND ATHLETE

General motor ability assumes **one overall ability**. A person with **good general motor ability** would be able to perform a **large number** of skills well. This concept has **not** been proven.

Specific motor ability assumes that **different sports** require **different motor abilities**. Each motor ability has little direct relation to any other motor ability. Just because a person is skilled in one activity it does not mean they will be skilled in all others. This concept is generally held as being **true**.

Why then do all-round athletes exist ?

- ❑ **Parental support** to develop excellence.

- ❑ **Cultural pressure** for good sporting performance.

- ❑ **Body size.**
  Large strong performers could have an advantage at a number of sports.

- ❑ **Personality traits**.
  A performer with a "sporting personality" would try hard and could do well at any sport.

- ❑ **Simple skills** may involve **general motor ability** .
  For example, hitting or jumping could be seen as general motor skills which could be transferred between activities.

Chapter 2 - Skill

Skill Classification
Gross v Fine Skills
Self Paced v Externally Paced Skills
Discrete v Continuous v Serial Skills
Closed v Open Skills

Chapter 2 - Skill

SKILL CLASSIFICATION

GROSS versus FINE SKILLS

Gross motor skill :   movement involving large muscle groups (walking, running, dead lift)

Fine motor skills :   movement involving small muscle groups (writing, darts, playing
                                                                                           piano)

Gross ➤➤➤➤➤➤➤➤➤➤➤➤➤➤➤➤➤➤ **Fine**
        dead lift running   kicking a football badminton   darts

SELF PACED versus EXTERNALLY PACED SKILLS

Self paced :   the timing of the movement is determined by the performer.

Externally paced :   the timing of the movement is affected/controlled by external factors
                                (wind, weather, opponents).

Self paced ➤➤➤➤➤➤➤➤➤➤➤➤➤➤➤➤ **Externally paced**
        tennis serve   tennis receive of serve

DISCRETE versus CONTINUOUS versus SERIAL SKILLS

Discrete: A motor skill that has a clearly defined beginning and end point.
                    Discrete skills are usually simple skills of very short duration.

Continuous: A motor skill that has no clearly defined beginning or end point.
                      The skill could therefore be of short, medium or long duration.

Serial: A group of discrete skills joined together to make one complex skill or
                  a sequence of skills.

DISCRETE	**CONTINUOUS**	**SERIAL**
a jump	swimming	gym sequence
a throw, catch	cycling	complex dive
a punch, kick	jogging	triple jump
a simple dive	rowing	pole vault

2.1

CLOSED versus OPEN SKILLS

Closed: Skills which are not affected by the environment.

Open: Skills which are affected by the environment.

Open ➤ **Closed**

team game (outdoors)   team game (indoors)   individual skill (outdoors)   individual skill (indoors)

- ❑   **Closed** skills are those that **can be repeated** time and time again with little difference in the performance.

- ❑   **Closed** skills are self **paced**.

- ❑   **Closed** skills need the performer to **concentrate** on **kinaesthetic feedback** concerning how a movement felt.

- ❑   **Practicing** for **closed** skills involve **repetitive** practice of **set skills** and routines.

- ❑   **Open** skills are **difficult** to **repeat** because **external factors** cannot be controlled.

- ❑   **Open** skills are **externally** paced.

- ❑   **Open** skills need **the performer** to make **decisions** concerning an ever **changing environment**.

- ❑   Practicing for **open** skills involves **varied practice** of different skills in different situations.

- ❑   When **learning** a difficult **open** skill it may be of benefit to **simplify** the skill. This can be achieved by making the skill more **closed** (reduce external effects).
  For example , reduce opposition or reduce the potential for variation.

Chapter 3 - Learning

Theories relating to the Learning of Skills
Classical Conditioning
Operant Conditioning
Trial and Error
Reinforcement
Positive and Negative Reinforcement
Punishment
When and How to Use Reinforcement and Punishment

Chapter 3 - Learning

THEORIES RELATED TO THE LEARNING OF SKILLS

If the learner is faced with a sporting problem and he/she comes up with a correct solution, the coach will probably praise him/her. The learner could in the future therefore connect his/her achievement of a correct performance with the receiving of praise. If the learner is faced with the same problem or situation, he/she will therefore probably produce the same response. The connection between a particular stimulus (problem, action or event) and a particular response is called the Stimulus-Response bond or **S-R** bond.

Teachers and coaches often try to use **S-R** bond theory to try and make their athletes respond to sporting situations ina particular way.

CLASSICAL CONDITIONING

- ❑ **Classical conditioning** is concerned with the **stimulus-response** bond.

- ❑ The **performer does not make a decision** towards the stimulus, all **responses** are **automatic**.

- ❑ It is very difficult to teach classical conditioning since most sporting situations require some element of **choice**. **Classical conditioning** could be taught **through set drills and practices** which connect **particular stimuli** to **particular responses**.

    For example, teacher blows whistle (**stimulus**)
            students sit down and are quiet (**response**)

            a defender is pressurised by an attacker (**stimulus**)
            defender sends the ball off the pitch (**response**).

- ❑ **Reinforcement** is necessary to strengthen the **S-R** bond.

- ❑ Learning using set drills may be quick but does not ensure that students understand.

OPERANT CONDITIONING

❑ **Operant conditioning** is concerned with the stimulus-**organism**-response bond.

❑ The learner can chose the response towards a **particular** stimulus as there are a **number of choices**.

❑ The teacher wants the performer to pick the correct response to a stimulus and makes sure this happens by **rewarding** the performer for connecting the correct response to the stimulus and **punishing** the performer when the wrong connection is made.

❑ The learner makes decisions based on the **idea** that **particular responses** will be **rewarded**.

❑ The learner may not know **why** the response is correct only that it will be **rewarded**.

❑ Teaching for operant conditioning must include **positive reinforcement and reward**. This is the main way the **S-R** bond is strengthened. Learning may take place through trial and error.

TRIAL AND ERROR

❑ This involves trying to link a correct response to a stimulus.
For example, in badminton, your opponent plays overhead clear to your midcourt (stimulus), then after experimentation you find the best return would be to smash (response).

❑ When teaching through trial and error the teacher must try to strengthen the **S-R** bond:

♦ use **positive reinforcement** to strengthen correct response.

♦ provide **feedback** to ensure the performer knows **what** is successful, and **how** success was achieved.

♦ teacher needs to give the performer enough **time** to work through the trial and error process.

♦ teacher must **not** make learning **too over repetitive**. This will lead to boredom, fatigue and reduced motivation therefore weakening the **S-R** bond.

REINFORCEMENT

This section is concerned with how a coach can make a **performer repeat correct** performance.

Magill (1989)   "**Reinforcement** is any action or event that **increases** the **probability** of a **response** occurring again."

POSITIVE AND NEGATIVE REINFORCEMENT

- ❑ Examples of **positive reinforcement** are **praise** and **rewards**. If a performer receives praise or rewards they are more likely to repeat the act in expectation of future rewards.

- ❑ **Negative reinforcement** is the **removal** of praise when performance is **incorrect**. A performer wants to be rewarded, if they are not they will change their performance in order to increase the chances of being rewarded.

- ❑ **Negative reinforcement** can also involve the coach **scolding incorrect** performance and **saying nothing when performance is correct**. The performer will want to avoid being scolded and will try to achieve correct performance.

- ❑ **Thordike's Law of Effect**: behaviour that is positively reinforced is liable to be repeated (coaches should therefore use positive reinforcement).

PUNISHMENT

Magill (1989)   "**Punishment** is any action or event that **decreases** the **probability** of a **response** occurring again."

- ❑ Punishment is **different** from reinforcement.

- ❑ **Reinforcement** tells the performer **what** to do.

- ❑ **Punishment** tells the performer **what not** to do.

- ❑ Consequently **reinforcement** is more **useful** than punishment.

- ❑ **Praise** is also better than punishment because punishment can lead to **negative** feelings such as **anxiety** and **resistant behaviour**.

WHEN AND HOW TO USE REINFORCEMENT AND PUNISHMENT

- ❑ Reinforcement and punishment only work if they have an **important effect** on the performer or if the performer **perceives** the effect to be **important** (if the coach is not respected the reinforcement will be of no value).

- ❑ **Reinforcement** or **punishment** must occur as **soon as possible** after the **behaviour** (which is seen to be **correct** or **incorrect** respectively) if it is to be effective.

- ❑ If reinforcement is **over used** it loses its value.

- ❑ **Reinforcement** should only be used when observing **correct behaviour**.

Chapter 4 - Motor Programme Theory

Motor and Executive Programmes
Motor Programme Theory
Open Loop Theory
Limitations of Open Loop Theory
Closed Loop Theory
Differences between Open and Closed Loop Theories
Teaching for Open and Closed Loop Theories
Hierarchies of Control
Executive Programmes and Subroutines
Executive Programmes and Subroutines in More Detail
Importance to the Teacher

Chapter 4 - Motor Programme Theory

MOTOR AND EXECUTIVE PROGRAMMES

MOTOR PROGRAMME THEORY

Motor programme theory is closely related to **open loop theory**. These theories look at how the **brain controls movement**.

OPEN LOOP THEORY

Open loop theory is concerned with the **sending of information**.

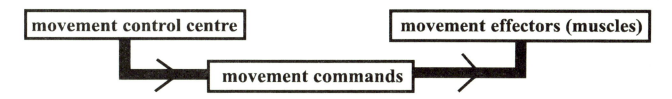

According to **open loop theory :**

-   A **decision** to make a movement is made by the **movement control centre**.
-   All the necessary information is sent in one big **chunk** (movement commands).
-   The information is received by the **effector organs** which carry out the movement.
-   **Feedback** is available but does **not** control movement.
-   Because of this, **changes cannot be made during** the movement

For example , in a golf swing , the brain assesses the situation, sends commands to the muscles concerning how to make the swing, then muscles carry out the commands.

LIMITATIONS OF OPEN LOOP THEORY

❑   According to **Schmidt** the brain **cannot store** millions upon millions of separate motor programs. In addition the brain cannot cope with new movements for which it does not have a motor program.

❑   Open loop theory explains **fast movements** well but **cannot** explain **slow positioning movements** where it is apparent that the performer is able to change a movement half way through a motor program.

CLOSED LOOP THEORY

Closed loop theory is concerned with the importance of **feedback**.

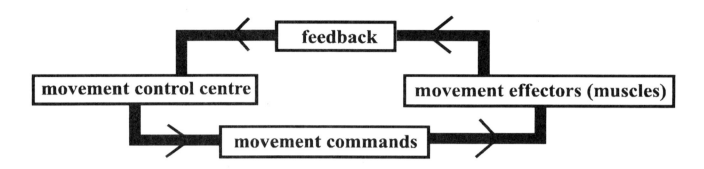

According to **closed loop theory** :

❑   A decision to make a movement is made by the **movement control centre.**
❑   Only **some** of the information necessary to make the movement is sent to the **effector organs**.
❑   The rest of the information is sent **during** the movement. The amount and type of information sent depends on **feedback** received during the movement.
❑   Because of this changes can be made **during** the movement

For example , riding a bike. The brain sends some messages to the muscles concerning how to ride. The muscles send messages back to the brain. When the brain detects any errors in balance it sends further commands to the muscles to rectify the imbalance.

DIFFERENCE BETWEEN OPEN AND CLOSED LOOP THEORY

❑   According to **closed loop** theorists, **feedback** can be used **during** movement. Movements can be **changed** at any time.

❑   According to **open loop** theorists, feedback **cannot** be used during movement, only afterwards. Once the commands have been sent the movement **cannot** be changed until the commands have been **carried out.**

❑   **Open loop** theory best explains **fast** movements where there is no time to react to feedback.
        For example , throwing , hitting and catching fast moving objects, jumping.

❑   **Closed loop** theory best explains **slower** movements where there is time to react to feedback .
        For example , positioning movements, hitting and catching slow moving objects.

TEACHING FOR OPEN AND CLOSED LOOP THEORIES

❑　　For **closed loop** movements the teacher will need to provide the learner with **feedback** which should include knowledge of performance and knowledge of results. The learners own kinaesthetic feedback can be enhanced by the teacher asking how the movement felt.

Teaching for **open loop** theory is concerned with :

❑　　Providing the learner with **enough information**

❑　　Helping the learner to send the information in the **correct order** (the timing of the movement).

This can be achieved by :

❑　　Providing large amounts of **varied practice**. This increases **movement memory** and so increases the chance of the **correct** motor commands being sent when performing a new skill.

❑　　Learning skills in **parts** to give the learner an idea of which **order** to run the parts (subroutines) of the skill. This will help to improve **timing**.

In the **early** stages of learning :

❑　　There is no spare **attentional capacity**, consequently, it is difficult for the learner to use ongoing feedback during the movement.

❑　　It can be assumed at this stage, that learning could be best explained using **open loop** theory.

In the **later** stages of learning :

❑　　When spare attentional capacity **is available**, the learner could use ongoing **feedback**. At this stage learning could be explained using **both** theories.

4.3

EXECUTIVE PROGRAMMES AND SUBROUTINES

To understand how motor programmes are formed one must examine **hierarchies of control.**

HIERARCHIES OF CONTROL

❑   A **hierarchy** is an order usually arranged in a pyramid shape.
         For example , the hierarchy of a school or company.

❑   A movement or **sequence of movements** can be arranged in a hierarchy.

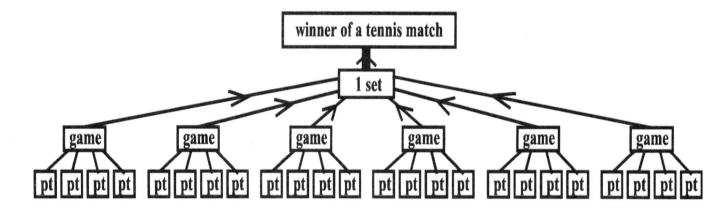

1.   To be a winner, the performer must win a set. To win a set, 6 games must be won. To win a game, 4 points must be won.

2.   To win a point, the rally must be won. To win the rally, a number of shots must be played.

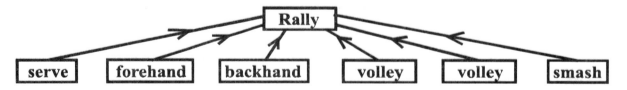

3.   To play each stroke, the performer must have mastered the points of correct stroke production.

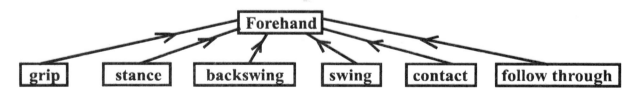

4. As a consequence, in order to be a winner, the basics must have been fully learned. Only then can the performer move onto the next step of the hierarchy.

EXECUTIVE PROGRAMMES AND SUBROUTINES

❑   Executive programs and subroutines explain hhow a performer is able to move from learning simple skills to performing **complex sequences** of movements.

❑   The **executive program** is the overall **plan of action** (the top row in the hierarchy)

❑   The **subroutines** are the **small parts** that make up the eceutive program (the lower rows of the hierarchy

❑   As the subroutines become learned, more and more subroutines become **automatic.** This gives the performer **spare attentional capacity** to try and learn more skills (the next row up in the hierarchy)

First learning stage :

(E.P.)

(subroutines)

Second learning stage :

(E.P.)

(subroutines)

❑   Once the performer learns the forehand, he/she becomes good enough to put it into a rally. What once was an executive program (forehand), now becomes a subroutine of a more **complex** executive program.

❑   According to **Robb**, subroutines are **"has-been" executive programs**. A skill can be a subroutine for an experienced performer and an executive program for the learner.

❑   It can be seen that we learn skills in **stages**. We must fully learn the first stage before moving on to a second.

EXECUTIVE PROGRAMMES AND SUBROUTINES IN MORE DETAIL

- ❏ Executive programs decide the **order** of the subroutines. They make decisions and are flexible.

- ❏ Subroutines are **fixed** and run off **automatically**. They can be changed if the executive program is changed.

- ❏ The learner's subroutines are liable to be **less specific** than those of a skilled performer and, as a consequence, will probably be inappropriate or ineffective.

IMPORTANCE TO THE TEACHER

- ❏ According to **Fitts** and **Posner**, adults learn new skills by **reorganising** existing subroutines. This implies that the performance of new skills is dependent on previously learned subroutines. The early years (between 8 and 12) have been seen as a very important time for skill learning. Subroutines learned during this time can have a great effect later on in life. It is therefore very important that early skills are **learned correctly**.

- ❏ To be able to move on to more complex skills, the learner must first develop a number of **varied** subroutines. The learner cannot learn new and different skills if he/she does not have a similar subroutine to draw on.

- ❏ The teacher must ensure that the young learner develops a wide variety of **correctly** learned subroutines.

- ❏ The executive program is concerned with the correct timing or **sequence** of the subroutines. It is important that the subroutines are learned in the correct order.

- ❏ The teacher must suggest the **order** in which the parts of a skill should be learned and devise practices which will enable the subroutines to **fit together** smoothly.

Chapter 5 - Schema Theory

Schema Theory
The Formation of Schema
Recall Schema
Initial Conditions
Response Specifications
Recognition Schema
Movement Outcomes
Sensory Outcomes
Conclusions

Chapter 5 - Schema Theory

SCHEMA THEORY

Following Schmidt :

❑   A **Schema** is a block of **stored information** needed to make a decision or movement.

❑   Movements are the **result** of motor programs.

❑   A **motor program** contains **all** the information needed to make a movement.
For example , which muscles to use, the order of the muscles to be used, the phasing of the muscle's contraction, or the time interval between each contraction.

❑   According to Schmidt **the brain cannot store** millions upon millions of **separate motor programs**. In addition **the brain cannot cope** with **new** movements for which it does not have a motor program.

❑   Instead of separate motor programs for every movement, Schmidt asserts that motor programs are grouped together to form **generalised motor programs**.
For example , a generalised motor program would deal with jumping, throwing, kicking, or lifting.

❑   An **advantage** of this grouping (into generalised motor programs) would be that the **brain does not have to store** so many programs, and any **new** movement can probably be executed by running a **generalised motor program** which **closely matches** the requirements of the **new** movement.

❑   The bigger the generalised motor program the more **efficient** the movement.

❑   Large amounts of varied practice are needed to improve or strengthen the schema.
(i.e. **Increase the size** of the generalised motor program).

❑   **Feedback** is important as it is used to correct and update the schema.

❑   When performing a new task the performer needs to use information from **previous similar tasks**. Errors are helpful because the bigger the bank of old information the bigger the chance of selecting the correct response for the new task.

❑   **Errors** are helpful because they help to strengthen the schema.
For example , in canoeing, how does the canoeist know how far they can lean before the canoe capsizes ? The canoeist knows because he/she has capsized accidentally before.

5.1

THE FORMATION OF SCHEMA

Information used to form schema :

- ❑ **Initial Conditions**   (Information concerning the environment)
- ❑ **Response Specifications** (Information concerning how to perform a movement)
- ❑ **Movement Outcomes**   (Information concerning the success or failure of the movement)
- ❑ **Sensory Consequences**   (Information concerning how the movement felt or looked like)

There are two types of schema **: recall schema** and **recognition schema.**

RECALL SCHEMA (initial conditions and response specifications)

- ❑ A **recall schema** refers to all information that is needed **before** a motor program is selected and run.

- ❑ A **recall schema** is formed when the **initial conditions** are **combined** with the **movement parameters** to initiate a motor program.

INITIAL CONDITIONS (environmental information)

- ❑ **Where** are; teamates, opposition, the goal ?
- ❑ **What** are; the playing conditions, weather ?
- ❑ What is the **condition** of; the car, horse, boat ?

RESPONSE SPECIFICATIONS (what to do)

- ❑ How much **speed** is needed ?
- ❑ How much **force** is needed ?
- ❑ How big should the **movement size** be ?
- ❑ Which **technique** to use ?

RECOGNITION SCHEMA (movement outcomes and sensory consequences)

❑   A **recognition schema** refers to all the information needed to **correct faulty performance** and **remember correct performance**.

❑   During and after any performance the schema is strengthened by **2 types of information**.

1) Movement Outcomes (success or failure)

❑   What was the **result** of the performance; how far, how fast, how well, how many ?

2) Sensory Consequences

❑   How did the performance **look, feel, sound** ?

❑   Information from movement outcomes and sensory consequences is **combined** to form the Recognition Schema. If the performance was **correct** it needs to be **remembered**, if it was **incorrect**, **adjustments** will be made to **movement parameters**.

CONCLUSIONS

❑   According to Schmidt, a **recall schema** is used for quick ballistic movements when there is **not enough time** to process **feedback**. A **recognition schema** is used for **evaluating performance**, or for producing **slow movements** when there **is enough time** to process **feedback**.

❑   Schema theory can be used to explain **all** movement. Closed loop theory can only account for **slow** movements, whilst open loop theory can only explain **fast** movements.

Chapter 6 - Information Processing

Information Processing
The Simple Model
The More Complicated Model
SENSORY INPUT
Important Factors Concerning Sensory Input
PERCEPTION
Attention
Limited Attentional Capacity Theories
The Single Channel Theory
The Multiple Channel Theory
Teaching for Attention
MEMORY
Short Term Sensory Store
Short term Memory or Working Memory
Long Term Memory
Memory and Performance
How to Improve Memory , a Coach's Guide
DECISION MAKING
Reaction Time
Hick's Law
The Psychological Refractory Period
Anticipation
How to Anticipate / Reduce Reaction Time
Mental Practice or Mental Rehearsal
Uses of Mental Rehearsal
FEEDBACK
Types of Feedback - Intrinsic and Extrinsic
Functions of Extrinsic Feedback
Problems with Feedback

Chapter 6 - Information Processing

INFORMATION PROCESSING

What happens if you want to make a movement ?

THE SIMPLE MODEL

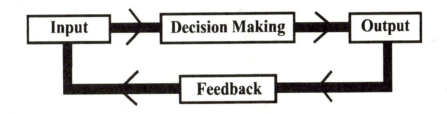

❑   **Input** is information entering the body from the senses.

❑   **Decision making** occurs in the brain.

❑   **Output** is the actual movement.

❑   **Feedback** is information concerning the movement.

For example , a cricket ball could be bowled on a line to hit the stumps (input), the batsman decides to play a defensive shot (decision making), he then plays a defensive shot (output), but hears the ball hit the stumps (feedback).

THE MORE COMPLICATED MODEL

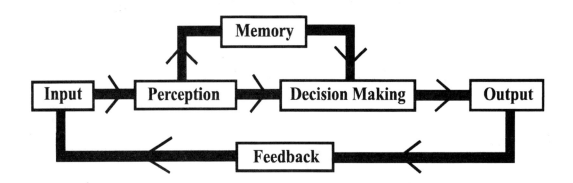

❑ **Input** is information entering the body from the senses.
❑ **Perception** occurs in the brain. It is the process whereby the sensory input is given meaning.
❑ **Memory** is used in a number of ways. At the perception stage memory is used to compare present sensory input to past sensory input in order for the performer to understand what is going on. Memory is also used at the decision making stage. Memories are used to compare what has happened in similar situations.
❑ **Decision making** occurs in the brain.
❑ **Output** is the actual movement.
❑ **Feedback** is information concerning the movement.

For example , when playing netball :

❑ You see your goal shooter get free of her marker. Goal attack is also free.(**input**).

❑ You perceive that goal attack is not ready to receive a pass.

❑ You perceive that goal shooter is ready to receive a pass (**perception** and **memory**).

❑ You use memory to help you decide what to do, and decide to use a bounce pass to the goal shooter player (**decision making** and **memory**).

❑ The appropriate motor commands are sent to the muscles and the movement is made (**output**).

❑ The pass is made and is successful (**feedback**).

SENSORY INPUT

Sensory input is **information** received through the senses : **Sight** (vision)   **Sound** (audition)
Feel (kinaesthesis)   **Smell** (olfaction)
Taste

IMPORTANT FACTORS CONCERNING SENSORY INPUT

For an improvement in performance it is no good simply practising, the teacher needs to **use** and **manipulate sensory information**.

The Hawthorne Effect

❑   According to **Hawthorne**, performance changes for the better when **changes** are made to the **learning** or performing **environment**. Hence pupils get bored if the teacher uses the same drills from lesson to lesson. Make the lessons varied, make them more interesting.

Selective Attention

❑   The **brain** can only cope with a certain amount of information, it **has a limited attentional capacity**. It is important that the brain selects the correct sensory information to attend to. The teacher needs to direct the pupil to attend to the relevant cues and disregard the irrelevant cues.

❑   This could be done by the teacher **changing the visual display** of the pupil to make it easier for him/her to selectively attend.
For example , two-tone cricket balls make spin easier to identify , or a newly painted hockey ball stands out more on a pitch.

❑   At the early or **cognitive** stage of learning, **visual feedback** is most important. In the **later** stages of learning, **kinaesthetic feedback** becomes more important. Consequently the teacher should ask the pupil how the movement felt, in an attempt to improve kinaesthetic memory.

Feedback

❑   Sensory information provides the pupil with **knowledge of performance** and **knowledge of results** which function to motivate, reinforce and direct behaviour. The teacher needs to let the pupil see how well he/she has performed.

Simulators and Trainers

❑   This is a way of learning **away from the real situation**, which could be **safer** and **speed up learning**. The practice **environment** can be **controlled** to help the learner to perceive his/her sensory information more effectively and quicker. Examples of the use of this idea are : windsurfer trainers, cricket catching cradles, scrummaging machines and golf simulators.

PERCEPTION

Perception can be explained as the way **sensory information is given meaning** so that we **understand** what is going on around us.

Major concepts :   **Attention   Memory**

ATTENTION

- ❑   **Attention** is related to the **amount of information** we can cope with.

- ❑   The amount of information we can attend to is limited. We have **limited attentional capacity.**

- ❑   Because of **limited attentional capacity** it is important that the performer attends to the **relevant cues** (important information), and disregards the irrelevant cues (unimportant information). This is known as **selective attention**.

- ❑   When the learner reaches the final stage of learning - the **autonomous stage**, some parts of performance become **automatic**. As a consequence we do not need to attend to those parts. This gives the performer **spare attentional capacity**.

- ❑   **Spare attentional capacity** will allow the performer to **attend to new elements** of a skill such as tactics or anticipating the moves of an opponent.

- ❑   The teacher needs to get the performer to the **autonomous stage of learning**. Once there, the teacher needs to help the performer make best use of their **spare attentional capacity** by identifying tactical components and helping them to **anticipate**.

- ❑   The teacher will also need to help the performer to **concentrate**, to **focus the attention** of the performer and to reduce the chance of **attentional switching** to unimportant information.

LIMITED ATTENTION CAPACITY THEORIES

These theories attempt to answer the questions:

- ❑ **How much can we attend to ?**
- ❑ **Can we attend to more than one thing at a time?**

THE SINGLE CHANNEL THEORY (Broadbent 1958)

- ❑ We can only **attend** to **one thing at a time**.
- ❑ Information gets processed **sequentially**, one item at a time, one item after another.
- ❑ Some theorists believe there is some form of attentional switching that allows the performer to monitor and react to different informational stimuli. This gives the **impression** of being able to attend to **two things at once**. In reality it's still only one thing at a time. An example of this would be the cocktail party effect, in which attention is apparently being paid to several conversations at once.
- ❑ Theorists suggest that the only way two things can be attended to at the same time is if they require a **small amount** of attentional capacity. Two pieces of simple information would be small enough to pass along the single channel.

THE MULTIPLE CHANNEL THEORY (Kahneman 1973)

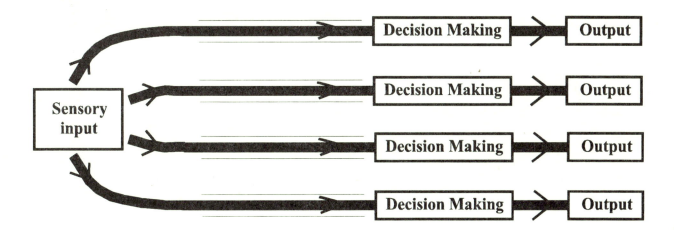

- ❑ So long as the incoming information comes along **different** channels, the performer could complete **more than one task**.
- ❑ An advanced games player will not need to attend to a large amount of information because certain actions are **automatic**. Spare attentional capacity can be used to attend to more than one task.
- ❑ **Effort** is perceived as taking up attentional capacity. A **skilled player** will be able to attend to a **second task** since the **amount** of **effort** expended on the first task could be **minimal**.

TEACHING FOR ATTENTION

The **brain** can only **attend** to a **limited amount of information**. It is important that the performer attends to the **relevant** information and **disregards irrelevant** information. This process is known as **selective attention**. Attention and selective attention can be improved in a number of ways.

❑ **Reduce the attentional demands during skill learning**

Skills are often learnt more quickly if they are broken down into **parts**. This enables the learner to fully concentrate on the most important parts of the skill and prevents him/her from becoming overloaded with information and so confused.

For example , the lay-up in basketball can be broken down into the running dribble, the one-two step, the jump, and the release.

❑ **Ensure basic skills are learned to the autonomous stage before progressing to more advanced skills.**

If the learner can **automatically** produce the **first** or **easy parts** of a skill, this will "free-up" **spare** attentional capacity which can be used to solve **more difficult** skill problems. Often, learners are stuck on so called learning plateaux, unable to move on because they do not have the attentional capacity which will enable them to make further progress.

❑ **Do not overload the learner with information**

Too many cues from the teacher or environment will **overload** the learner. The teacher needs to reduce the cues by controlling the environment

For example :
      i) learning in semi-opposed situations rather than fully opposed,
      ii) teaching instructions kept to a minimum.

The teacher must also highlight the cues that are important, suggesting to the learner what he/she should be attending to.

❑ **Do not underload the learner** .

Too little information will underload the system leading to **inattentiveness** and loss of motivation.

❑ **Selective attention and stage of learning**

At the **early** stages of learning, **visual** information is most important. Consequently the teacher should instruct the learner to attend to the most important visual cues. **Later, kinaesthetic** information becomes more important. Consequently the teacher should instruct the learner to attend to how the movement felt.

❑ **Improve concentration**

♦ Pupils must learn how to **concentrate** on the **relevant** cues and disregard the irrelevant cues if they are to fully use their attentional capacity.

♦ The teacher must **retain** the learner's **interest** by **introducing new tasks**, and by making existing tasks more challenging.

♦ **Positive reinforcement** should be used when correct performance is observed, **negative reinforcement** and **punishment** should also be used when appropriate to ensure **maximum** concentration.

❑ **The effects of arousal levels on attentional capacity**

♦ **Arousal levels** have an effect on attentional capacity.

♦ **Too much** arousal can **reduce** attentional capacity.

♦ Being over-aroused can cause **narrowing of the attentional field**, and can be likened to a games player wearing blinkers.

♦ This is detrimental to some sports where players **need to be aware** of everything going on around them. For example , a quarterback in American Football.

♦ Conversely for sports that have small attentional demands, it is a bonus to be able to **shut out unwanted interference**. For example , weight lifting.

♦ **Too little arousal** can also **reduce attentional capacity**. It is important for the teacher or coach to make certain that his/her athletes perform with the appropriate level of arousal for their activity.

MEMORY

" The capacity that permits organisms to **benefit** from their **past experiences**."

The 3 types of memory are :

- ❏ **Short term sensory store STSS**
- ❏ **Short term memory STM**
- ❏ **Long term memory LTM**

SHORT TERM SENSORY STORE (STSS)

- ❏ **All** information from the senses is passed through the **STSS**.
- ❏ Information is **kept** for up to **1 second**.
- ❏ If the information is **not considered important** it is lost and **forgotten** and replaced by new information.

SHORT TERM MEMORY OR WORKING MEMORY

The 3 major characteristics of **STM** are :

Duration

- ❏ This is the amount of **time** new information is kept before being lost.
- ❏ It lasts between **20-30 seconds** before we lose the information.
  For example , a new telephone number.

Capacity

- ❏ This can be explained as how **much** information we can remember.
- ❏ As a rule, **7 items, + or - 2** items. This can be improved by "chunking" information, placing it into easily remembered groups.
  For example , 768594032 becomes 768 594 032.

Processing

- ❏ This relates to **how** the information is used.
  For example, the information can be used to solve a problem or to accomplish a task, or it can be stored in the long term memory for future use.

LONG TERM MEMORY (LTM)

❑ Long term memory is a **store of past experiences** which have been very well learned.

❑ **LTM** is limitless and once in **LTM**, information is **not forgotten**.

❑ Just because information is in **LTM** does not mean it is easily recalled. Information is coded and the performer must be able to **connect the memory to the code** before they can recall the memory.

The three main parts of **LTM** are :

Procedural Memory

❑ This is information about **how to do** something i.e. the correct procedure, or order in which tasks are to be completed. The procedural memory serves as a "blueprint" when you need to repeat a movement, a sort of recall schema.

Semantic Memory

❑ This is a **knowledge** memory.
❑ General facts and concepts are stored here. If the procedural memory is the "how", the semantic memory is the "what".

   For example , knowledge of football trivia or concepts such as the sweeper system and offside trap.

Episodic Memory

❑ This is knowledge about personally experienced events.
      For example your first kiss!

MEMORY AND PERFORMANCE

❑ Select a **relevant** performance goal, (for example saving a penalty).

❑ Use information from the **STM** to assess your opponent's actions.
For example , in soccer, the way the player runs towards the ball, the angle the kicking foot makes with the ball and so on.

❑ Compare present information from **STM** with past experience (**LTM**) before deciding what to do. **Episodic** memory provides examples of what this and other players have done in the past. **Semantic** memory provides information on what you should do in the situation. **Procedural** memory provides information on how to perform the selected skill.

❑ Carry out the desired skill.

HOW TO IMPROVE MEMORY, A COACH'S GUIDE

To improve memory, information needs to be transferred from **STSS** to **STM** to **LTM** as **quickly** as possible.

❑ Instructions need to be **clear and concise**. Too much information and the performer will forget.

❑ Provide **lots of practice**.
Well learned tasks are more easily transferred to **LTM**. Skills must therefore be overlearned.

❑ **Speed** of learning.
Things that are learned quickly are more likely to be forgotten.

❑ Information is most easily remembered in **picture** form, so try to use examples that enable the performer to picture the correct technique/tactic.
For example , "the toilet position" gives a mental picture of the body position needed when setting up a rugby maul.

❑ Use **phrases** and **sayings** which can be easily **remembered**.
For example , "chin-knee-toe", when describing the alignment of body parts during the preparation phase of the shot putt.

❑ The **Von Restorf** effect. Any information that is presented in an **unusual** way will be remembered. Make a performance out of teaching, make it different and interesting.

DECISION MAKING

Relevant concepts here are :
- ❑ **Reaction Time**
- ❑ **Anticipation**
- ❑ **Mental Rehearsal**

The coach will try to **improve decision making** by helping to make the performer make decisions quicker by improving reaction time, and developing the performer's ability to anticipate the moves of an opponent.

REACTION TIME

" The amount of time between a stimulus and the first movement initiated in response to the stimulus."

For example , the reaction time at the start of a sprint race would be the time between the gun going off and the start of pressure being applied to the starting blocks.

Response time = reaction time + movement time (time taken to complete the action)

Types of Reaction Time :

❑   **Simple reaction time**

The time between a single stimulus and one response.
For example , response to the starter's gun.

❑   **Choice reaction time**

The time between one of several stimuli and the response to this chosen stimulus.
The correct stimulus must be chosen and then responded to.
For example , a bowler (in cricket, softball or baseball) could bowl a different line and length. The batter must identify the line and length before selecting a shot.

The **more choices** a person has the more information needs processing , the **longer it takes** to process the information, the **slower the reaction time**.

HICK'S LAW

❑ **Increasing** the **number** of **stimuli increases** the **reaction time**.

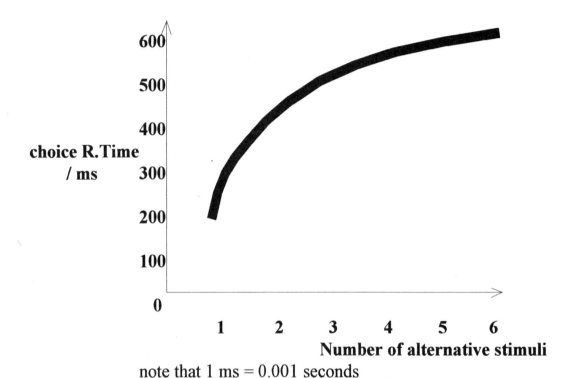

note that 1 ms = 0.001 seconds

❑ **Simple reaction time** may be about **200 ms**. But when the alternatives are increased to two the reaction time nearly **doubles** .

❑ **Hick's Law** is significant for sports players. A player should always try to keep their opponent **guessing** (and therefore providing a number of possible stimuli - only one of which would be the correct one) in an attempt to slow the opponent's reaction time. Vary play and do not be predictable.

THE PSYCHOLOGICAL REFRACTORY PERIOD (PRP)

❑   The **PRP** is the concept which could explain why a performer is unable to quickly respond to a **dummy** or **fake**. The **PRP** is the **time taken** to **react** to a **second stimulus after a first stimulus has occurred.**

❑   It refers to the **time taken to react** once an individual has **realised** he/she has responded in an incorrect way and want to **change** his/her response.

    For example , you react to an opponent's tennis shot by shaping to play a forehand, then you realise you should be playing a backhand.

❑   The **PRP** is the **time taken to change your mind.**

❑   In sport the **PRP** is generally the time it takes to respond to an opponent's fake or dummy.

❑   It happens because the brain has only a **limited ability** to **process information.** We have **difficulty** in dealing with **more than one stimulus at a time** so we **deal with the first stimulus before moving on to the second.**

❑   Our eyes may tell us that we have been faked (deceived) but we cannot do anything about it until the brain has **finished processing** the initial response.

    For example , a rugby player throws a dummy, the defender responds thinking that a pass is being made. The defender is then unable to attempt to tackle the attacker until the motor program for responding to a pass is finished.

❑   The **PRP** can be as much as **0.5 seconds**, so it is very important to use fakes and dummies in order to **slow down** the **reactions** of an **opponent**.

ANTICIPATION

" The ability to **predict future events** from **early signals** or **past events**."

For example , a goal keeper diving to save a penalty before the penalty has been taken.

Why Anticipate?

❑ Quick reaction times are often the difference between success and failure, reaction time can be speeded up if the performer **learns to anticipate** certain actions.

❑ Good performers start running motor programs **before** the stimulus is fully recognised. In other words, they **anticipate** the strength, speed and direction of a stimulus.

HOW TO ANTICIPATE / REDUCE REACTION TIME

❑ **Selectively attend** to the most important cues which will give you clues how to anticipate (for example , the position of an opponent's body or the direction in which he/she is look-ing).

   The coach should identify **which** cues to attend to.

❑ **Predict** an opponent's play by identifying consistencies in his/her play (for example , an opponent's favourite move or shot).

❑ Anticipation will also include the idea that an opponent may be using a **fake or dummy**. Be prepared, think for all eventualities.

❑ Remember your opponent will also be trying to anticipate.
   Try to slow their reactions by varying play or using fakes and dummies. You must try to **increase choice reaction time** in your opponent.

MENTAL PRACTICE OR MENTAL REHEARSAL

Definition: practice or rehearsal of a skill without actual physical movement.

Used by: skiers, golfers, athletes, tennis players, gymnasts

How: by watching a demonstration or film, reading or listening to instructions, imagining movements.

The Neuromuscular Explanation

❑   **Thinking** about **movement** actually produces **nerve impulses which fire in the correct order**.

❑   Consequently, mental practice is supposed to result in actual physical practice.

❑   There is little evidence to support this explanation, but it could be helpful in improving the quality if kinaesthetic feedback.

The Cognitive Explanation

❑   **Thinking** about **strategies and tactics** can help the performer make the **correct decisions** on the field.

❑   It is supposed to help the performer anticipate.

❑   In this way the performer is better able to understand skills and tactics.

The Confidence Explanation

❑   Mental rehearsal has been claimed to improve the **confidence** of performers which should lead to **improved motivation** and performance.

❑   It also readies the performer for action and stimulates both mental and physical faculties.

❑   It is like a mental warm up.

USES of MENTAL REHEARSAL

❑   In a potentially **dangerous situation** as a **safe** way of **practising**.

❑   To improve the **confidence** of performers who have lost or who have low confidence.

❑   To help **focus** the mind, as the performer is able to **imagine perfect performance** without harmful distractions.

FEEDBACK

" Any kind of **sensory information**, not just that concerning errors."

TYPES OF FEEDBACK

Intrinsic :   Feedback **during** the movement that the performer can perceive.

Extrinsic :   **Post performance** feedback.

For example : in a 100m race :

INTRINSIC	EXTRINSIC
sight: seeing other runners	knowledge of performance
sound: hearing opposition/crowd	knowledge of results
proprioception: feeling muscle tension	
smell	

Knowledge of Performance:

❑   Information about **performance** .

❑   (Technical information from a number of sources including the coach, information from video, film, newspaper)

Knowledge of Results:

❑   Information concerning the **outcome** .
    (for example , success or failure, distance or time).

❑   Information can be from a number of sources: from coach, video, newspapers and others

FUNCTIONS OF EXTRINSIC FEEDBACK

> ❑ **Motivational**
> ❑ **Reinforcing**
> ❑ **Informational**

Motivational

❑ **Information** concerning **success** and **failure** can be **motivational**. Success is motivational. Failure can act as a spur to motivate.

Reinforcing

❑ According to **Thorndike's Law of Effect**, behaviour that is rewarded will tend to be repeated.

❑ Positive and negative reinforcement will **increase the chance** of the performer repeating the performance.

> For example, if the performer is praised after correct performance the performer is liable to want to repeat the performance.

Informational

❑ Feedback provides information about **errors** and therefore provides the basis for error correction.

PROBLEMS WITH FEEDBACK

❑ Performers can become **dependent** on feedback.

❑ When it is **withdrawn**, performance can **deteriorate**.

❑ The **performer repeats performance** in order to receive **feedback**, once feedback is withdrawn there becomes no reason to repeat the performance.

❑ The coach should gradually **fade out feedback** in order to reduce the effects of feedback dependency.

Chapter 7 - Stages of Learning

Putting Learning Theories into Practice
Phases in Skill Learning
Cognitive Stage
Associative Stage
Autonomous Stage
Assessing Learning Using Learning Curves
Different Types of Learning Curves
A Beginner's Learning Curve During One Practice Session
How to Avoid Plateaux

Chapter 7 - Stages of Learning

PUTTING LEARNING THEORIES INTO PRACTICE

PHASES IN SKILL LEARNING - due to Fitts and Posner (1967)

In order to learn any new skill the learner will pass through **three** distinct phases before achieving mastery of the skill.

COGNITIVE STAGE (absolute beginner)

❑ The learner needs to know **what** to do.
- ♦ The learner needs to get a **mental picture** of the movement.
- ♦ The teacher should make good use of **demonstrations**.
- ♦ **Visual** information best helps the learner gain the mental picture.

❑ The teacher uses **verbal** cues to highlight the **correct sequencing** of the movement.
- ♦ For example , the teacher says "now" to initiate the correct timing of a particular movement.

❑ The learner has a **limited attentional capacity** to cope with information.
- ♦ Instructions should be brief and to the point.
- ♦ Too much information will only confuse the learner.

❑ As the learner has little idea of what is a correct performance, the teacher may have to use **physical guidance** and actually physically manipulate the learner's limbs into the correct position.

ASSOCIATIVE STAGE (fault correction)

❑ The learner now has an **overall picture** of what is required but still makes mistakes.

❑ The learner needs to know **how** to complete each **stage** of movement.
- · The teacher may break the skill into **parts** so that the learner can practice each part separately.

❑ The teacher will use **demonstration** to highlight correct technique and timing, and use **verbal feedback** to correct faults.

❑ The learner will also need **encouragement** from the teacher in order to maintain motivation.

AUTONOMOUS STAGE (automatic)

❑ The learner knows how to **complete** the skill and can do so with a great degree of competence and proficiency.

❑ The learner does not have to concentrate on performance and seems to perform **automatically**.

❑ The learner has **spare** attentional capacity and can now concentrate on other things.
  For example , within a team game, a player can now concentrate on tactics.

❑ The learner has **the ability to teach themselves**.
  ◆ The teacher can use quite complicated verbal feedback since the learner is capable of understanding it.

❑ The learner can make greater use of **kinaesthetic** information.
  ◆ The teacher should ask the learner to try and remember how the correct movement felt.

ASSESSING LEARNING USING LEARNING CURVES

Learning :   A change in performance which is exhibited through increased levels of consistency.

- ❑   Learning can be measured through **performance tests**.

- ❑   Test performance, practice, test again, practice, test again.

- ❑   If learning has taken place performance should have **improved**.

Below we have a graph showing performance against time for basketball free throws (10). The learner would take a test (in this case 10 basketball free shots) once per week. He/she would then practice this activity in between tests.

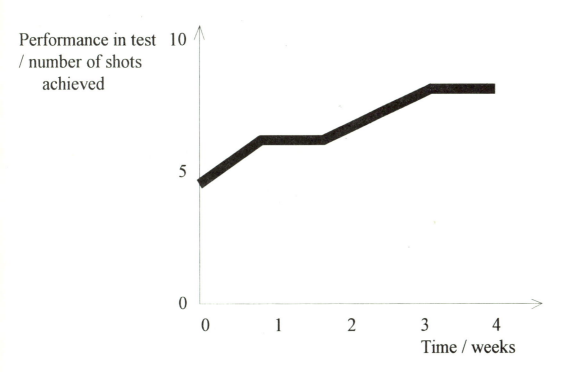

But, improvement in performance may **not** be as a **result** of learning, it may have been due to **external factors**, such as luck or the encouragement of co-competitors.

DIFFERENT TYPES OF LEARNING CURVES

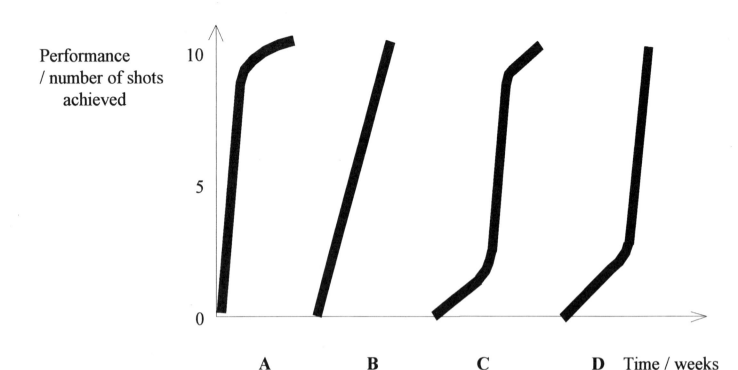

A   Steep curve which becomes more shallow with time.
A steep curve indicates quick learning, a shallow curve indicates slower learning.

B   Straight line, this indicates a constant and regular improvement in learning.

C   S shaped curve. Shallow, steep, then shallow.
Learning was relatively easy at first then became more difficult then became easy again.

D   Shallow curve which then steepens. Learning was relatively hard at first then became easier.

A BEGINNER'S LEARNING CURVE DURING ONE PRACTICE SESSION.

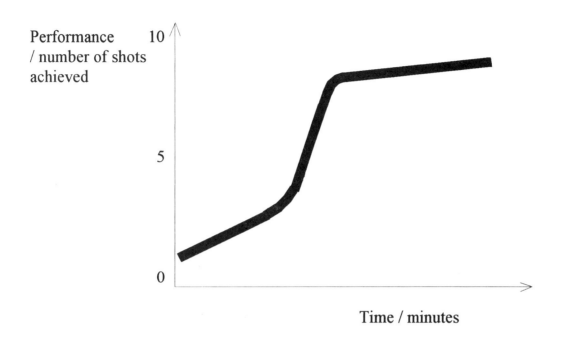

- At **first progress is slow** (shallow slope). The learner is still working out the requirements of the task.

- When the learner becomes aware of what is required, **performance improves greatly** (steep slope) and the learner is free to practice.

- At this point there is **no change in performance (plateau).** This may be due to lack of motivation or the performer suffering from fatigue.

HOW TO AVOID PLATEAUX

- Do **not** attempt skill learning when **fatigued**.

- **Motivation** levels must be maintained.

- **Selective attention** is important, performers must concentrate on the most important parts of the skill.

- The performer must be **capable** of performing the skill.

Chapter 8 - Transfer of Learning

The Theory of Transfer of Learning and its Application
Positive Transfer
Negative Transfer
Zero Transfer
Bilateral Transfer
Proactive Transfer
Retroactive Transfer
Stimulus and Response Generalisation
Stimulus Generalisation
Response Generalisation
Problems Associated with Generalisation
Teaching to Increase Positive Transfer and Reduce Negative Transfer
Factors Affecting the Amount of Transfer

Chapter 8 - Transfer of Learning

THE THEORY OF TRANSFER OF LEARNING AND ITS APPLICATION

Transfer of learning refers to the effect that learning one task has on the learning of another.

POSITIVE TRANSFER

❑ This theory indicates that **prior learning promotes present learning**.

❑ The learning of task 1 has a **beneficial effect** on the learning of task 2.
  For example , a tennis player could use prior learning when trying to learn the overhead serve in volleyball.

❑ The higher the degree of **similarity** between the parts of two separate tasks the greater the chance of positive transfer between the skills.

NEGATIVE TRANSFER

❑ In this case, **prior learning has an inhibiting effect on present learning**.

❑ The learning of task 1 has an **adverse effect** on the learning of task 2.
  For example , tennis players may find learning to play squash difficult since tennis is played with a firm wrist. To play squash you must learn to play with a flexible wrist action.

❑ Negative transfer is most likely to occur when a new response is required for an old stimulus.

For example , a basketballer when playing netball, may incur negative transfer when trying to respond to the new demands of netball using similar but inappropriate basketball skills.

  ♦ If the stimulus is requiring the player to defend the ball carrier, the old response would be to rush in and get within the three feet exclusion zone.

  ♦ The appropriate new response would be to defend from the required distance, the basketball player will find this difficult.

Another example , suppose that **a rugby player** has always been taught to fall to the ground when tackled in order for his team mates to set up a ruck.

  ♦ If the coach changes tactics and decides to play a mauling game it will be difficult for the player to stay standing in the tackle in order to set up a maul.

❑ Negative transfer effects are usually **temporary** and overcome with practice.

8.1

ZERO TRANSFER

- ❑ In this case, **prior learning has no effect on present learning**.
- ❑ The learning of task 1 has no effect on the learning of task 2.
  For example , football players would not be able to use their skills when learning to swim.

BILATERAL TRANSFER

- ❑ In this case, **learning can occur between limbs.**
- ❑ A skill that is learned with one limb can affect the learning of the same skill with the opposite limb.
- ❑ Bilateral transfer is generally between one arm and the other arm or from leg to leg.
  For example , throwing with either hand and kicking with either foot.
- ❑ The **cognitive explanation**. Thinking about a skill may improve transfer of that skill to an opposite limb.
- ❑ The **motor control explanation**. When learning a skill with the opposite limb the performer does not have to start from scratch. A **schema** already exists for the initial limb. The schema has only to be modified for the new limb.

PROACTIVE TRANSFER

- ❑ The effect that learning a skill has on a skill that **has not yet been learned**. The effect could be positive, negative or zero.

RETROACTIVE TRANSFER

- ❑ The effect that learning a skill has on a **previously learned skill**. The effect could be positive, negative or zero.

STIMULUS AND RESPONSE GENERALISATION

Stimulus and response generalisation is concerned with **the learning of generalised patterns of movement** rather than **situation specific** forms of movement. It is a form of **transfer** because the performer uses previously learned skills in new situations.

STIMULUS GENERALISATION

❑ According to classical conditioning. a particular **response** is connected to a particular **stimulus**.

  ◆ For example , a badminton student always plays an overhead clear to a shot played deep and high.

❑ **Stimulus generalisation** occurs when the response is **triggered** to **anything resembling** the original stimulus.

  ◆ In the example of the badminton student, she plays an overhead clear to any shot that is played above head height.

RESPONSE GENERALISATION

❑ **Response generalisation** theory suggests that once a response has been learned to a stimulus, a performer will react to the same stimulus by responding in a **number of similar but different ways.**

  ◆ For example , the cricket batter (once he has learnt how to defend his stumps) will learn how to play a number of shots to the same type of delivery.

PROBLEMS ASSOCIATED WITH GENERALISATION

❑ With stimulus generalisation a player's pattern of play becomes **predictable** and an opponent will find it easy to anticipate.

❑ Response generalisation does not give **precision** of movement.

❑ At high levels of sport it is important to be able **differentiate** between stimuli, and respond to each one **specifically**, otherwise negative transfer could occur.

  ◆ In the example of the cricket batter , he should play each delivery on its merit, and this will require learning specific shots to play against specific deliveries.

8.3

TEACHING TO INCREASE POSITIVE TRANSFER OF LEARNING AND REDUCE NEGATIVE TRANSFER OF LEARNING

❏ **Increase the similarity between the practice situation and game.**

Transfer is said to be greatest **between two tasks which are similar**. Practice situations must closely match competitive situations if transfer is to be maximised.

- ◆ Practice in **opposed** situations.
  For example , basketball shooting against opposition.
- ◆ **Include match day variables** into practice situation.
  For example , different weather conditions, playing surfaces, opposition tactics, crowd noise.

❏ **Make certain that the basics are fully learned.**

The basics provide the **foundation** for any transfer of learning. Even experienced players should practice the basics and not be allowed to slip into bad habits.

According to **Magill** " maximising practice on the original task is directly related to the likelihood of positive transfer to a subsequent task."

❏ **Increase the size and variability of the practice situation**

The sportsplayer is always faced with **different** and **new task** situations. The experienced player will be able to draw from a **large generalised motor program**. It is important to practice for every eventuality, so, when faced with a new situation, the performer should be able to transfer knowledge from a similar task.

For example , the cricket batter needs to learn how to face spin bowling and seam bowling, on different pitches and in different conditions.

❏ **Make the performer aware that transfer is possible**

Transfer of learning is only possible if the performer **realises** that he/she can transfer a previously learned skill to solve a new problem.

For example , the teacher would allow for transfer by telling the pupil that the overhead serve in volleyball is very similar to the serve in tennis.

❏   **Make certain the performer understands what is expected**

The performer needs to **understand** the **requirements** of the task so that he/she can get the task "**ordered**" in his/her mind. It is difficult to use transfer of learning if the performer has no idea of what needs to be achieved and how to achieve it.

❏   **Direct transfer of learning**

According to **Gestaltist** theory, direct transfer of learning between one sport and another can be best achieved by teaching the **principles common to both**. A number of different skills may have the same underlying principle.

For example , positioning in team games. The games are different, but the principle of width and depth in defence is the same for all games. Other principles for team games could include the concepts of support, keeping possession, going forward, and creating space.

FACTORS AFFECTING THE AMOUNT OF TRANSFER

❏   **Similarity between tasks**

You would expect a good **racquet** sports player to transfer those skills to a **batting** game or to **golf**. Conversely, a good swimmer would **not** have a lot of transfer to take to racquet sports.

❏   **Method of teaching**

A number of different teaching methods exist. Those which **make use of previously learnt similar skills** will enable the greatest transfer to take place.

For example , beating an opponent with a dribble in Hockey. The teacher says "Hockey is like Football, imagine the ball is a football and the stick is your leg, try to fake the defender one way and you go the other, just like you would do in Football." Hence transfer from football to hockey could be positive.

❏   **Bilateral transfer**

Transfer may well **increase** if a similar skill has been learnt with a **different** limb.

For example , learning to paint with your feet would be more difficult if you could not already do it with your hands.

❏   **Level of initial learning**

It has already been stated that **foundations** need to have been laid to ensure further learning. Those who have been taught the basic skills will be in a better position to transfer those skills to more advanced situations. Consequently, learning at an early age is very important.

❏   **Complexity and organisation**

Complexity refers to the **number of component parts to a skill**. A skill is said to be complex when it has a large number of component parts. **Organisation** is concerned with the interrelationships of the parts of a skill.

A skill that is **high in complexity** and **low in organisation** is best taught by making the performer practice **related but easier tasks first** then make it harder.

For example , dribbling a football around cones before trying to beat a player with a dribble.

A skill that is **low in complexity** and **high in organisation** (it has a large timing element) is best taught by making the performer practice **related but harder tasks first** then make it easier.

For example , in rifle shooting, make the target smaller at first.

8.6

Chapter 9 - Motivation

Motivation
Types of Motivation
Motivational Factors
Intrinsic or Extrinsic Motivation - Which is most Effective ?
Teaching for Motivation

Chapter 9 - Motivation

MOTIVATION

Motivation is :

- ❑ **Stallings (1966)** "An internal factor that arouses and directs behaviour."
- ❑ The **power** or **drive** behind why we do something.
- ❑ Responsible for:
    - ♦ the **selection** and **preference** for an activity,
    - ♦ the **persistence** at the activity,
    - ♦ the **intensity** and **effort** put into performance

Performance = Capabilities + Motivation

TYPES OF MOTIVATION

Intrinsic Motivation
- ❑ Described as feelings from **inside** ourselves.
    For example , fun, enjoyment, joy, satisfaction.

Extrinsic Motivation
- ❑ Described as feelings coming from gaining **external** rewards both physical (money, trophies) and emotional (praise).

Primary and Secondary Motivation
- ❑ **Primary** motivation is derived from the **activity itself.**
- ❑ **Secondary** motivation comes from **anything other than taking part.**
    For example , a performance undertaken to give pleasure to coach or friends, or to win medals.

Positive and Negative Motivation
- ❑ **Any** aspect of competing can have a **positive** or **negative** effect on motivation.
- ❑ **Winning** is **positively** motivating, **losing** can be **negatively** motivating.
- ❑ The **audience** can have both a positive or negative effect.

MOTIVATIONAL FACTORS (reasons why people perform)

Alderman and Wood (1976) Motivation Inventory :

- ❑ **Affiliation** (making friends)
- ❑ **Aggression** (intimidating)
- ❑ **Excellence**
- ❑ **Independence**
- ❑ **Power** (influencing others)
- ❑ **Stress** (excitement)
- ❑ **Success** (extrinsic rewards)

9.1

INTRINSIC OR EXTRINSIC MOTIVATION - WHICH IS MOST EFFECTIVE ?

❑ **Intrinsic motivation can outlast extrinsic motivation.**

◆ Athletes who are too old or unfit to win trophies, fame or money may still be able to enjoy sport.

◆ Once an athlete has won a gold medal, what else is there?
What better reason to do something than enjoyment?

❑ **The type of motivation required depends on the task.**

◆ **Margaret Clifford** (1972), "As task complexity increases intrinsic motivation increases." The **learning** of **complex** tasks is heavily **dependent** upon **intrinsic** motivation. Consequently **simple** tasks may be performed more often to a higher standard if **external** rewards are present.

◆ Tasks which athletes do not **wish** to complete (perhaps through risk of fear or injury) may be completed with the use of **extrinsic** rewards.

❑ **The regular use of extrinsic rewards may undermine intrinsic motivation.**

◆ Sport which is viewed as **play** can be transformed into **work** (and therefore have connotations of undue effort or fatigue) once financial rewards are given for performance. When the rewards are taken away there may no longer be any reason to take part.

❑ **Motivation is greatest when the athlete is in control of the situation.**

◆ **Situations** can be internally or externally controlled. If you do something because you **desire** to do it (**internal** control) your level of motivation will be higher than if you are **told** to do something (**external** control). **Extrinsic motivation can increase external control whilst intrinsic motivation can increase internal control.**

◆ Extrinsic motivation can transform **play** into **work**. The use of extrinsic rewards may increase external control. For example, the athlete who formerly trained for intrinsic reasons, becomes professional (extrinsic rewards are given for performance), and may be disinclined to train if payment ceased. His reason for training has been removed.

◆ **Rewards** should be used very **carefully**. They should be used as a means of **informing** the athlete how well he/she is doing **rather than the reason** to compete. They should be used to complement and heighten intrinsic motivation rather than as a controlling factor determining whether or not to do something.

TEACHING FOR MOTIVATION

❏ Find out the performer's **reason** to participate and **adapt** teaching methods to accommodate for it.
For example , if the performer is motivated by competition, make training more competitive.

❏ **Success** is motivating.
Ensure everyone gets their fair share of success.

❏ **Praise** is motivating.
Make certain correct behaviour is rewarded.

❏ **Play** itself is motivating.
Training sessions should include the opportunity to play.

❏ Similar training sessions can be boring.
Ensure training is **varied** and **different**.

❏ Each activity has an **optimum** level of motivation, for example , to compete in danger sports the performer must be highly motivated.
The teacher must be aware of the optimum level of motivation needed for any activity and try to help the performer achieve it.

❏ The **overuse** of **extrinsic** rewards can transform play into work when the performer starts to perceive the reward as being the **only reason to play**.

❏ Make the performer **seek high levels of achievement** by **increasing** his/her **need to succeed**.
The high achiever sets high yet achievable goals, is confident and positive and attributes success to his/her own skill.

9.3

Chapter 10 - Presentation of Skills

Presentation of Skills
Possible Methods
The Whole Method
The Part Method
Whole Part Whole Method
Progressive Part Method
Task Complexity and Task Organisation

Chapter 10 - Presentation of Skills

PRESENTATION OF SKILLS

❑   The teacher must decide whether to teach the entire skill or to break it down into parts and so that each part can be learned separately.

❑   The decision on **which** method is best depends on a number of factors including :

♦   the **personality** of the **learner**
♦   the level of **ability** of the **performer**
♦   the **facilities** and **time** available
♦   the **size** and **structure** (age, physique, gender) of the teaching **group**

POSSIBLE METHODS

❑   **whole learning**
❑   **part learning**
❑   **whole - part - whole learning**
❑   **progressive part learning**

THE WHOLE METHOD

❑   The **whole** method involves teaching a skill in its **entirety** without breaking it down onto parts.
❑   Generally if at all possible it is best to learn a skill using the whole method.

Advantages

♦   The learner appreciates the **end product**.
♦   The learner gets a feeling of the **timing** of the movement.
♦   The learner can understand the **relationship** between the **subroutines** of the skill.
♦   Learning is **quicker** because the learner does not have to learn how to put the parts together.

Disadvantages

♦   **Unsuitable** for **complex** skills.
♦   When the learner is at the **early stage** of learning they may **not** be able to cope with skills having **high attentional demands**.
♦   For **safety** reasons skills may have to be broken down into parts.

10.1

THE PART METHOD

❑   This involves breaking the skill into **parts** or **segments**. Each part is **practised separately** and then the parts are **joined together**.

Advantages

◆   Useful if the skill is **complex** as the learner can cope with small parts but not the whole.

◆   It can be **safer**. The danger element can be reduced.

◆   It allows the teacher to **focus** on particular **elements** if the skill. Learning in parts is **motivating**, since it gives small steps of success.

Disadvantages

◆   **Transfer** from part to whole may **not** be effective. It is **difficult** to split skills which are **highly organised** (the parts are linked together).

◆   **Reduces kinaesthetic** awareness.

◆   Learner **loses awareness** of the end product.

◆   **Continuity** of the skill is **lost**.

WHOLE - PART - WHOLE METHOD

❑   At **first** the **whole** skill is attempted.

❑   If **errors** are **apparent** then **those parts** of the skill that resulted in errors **are practised in isolation** before attempting the **whole** skill again.

PROGRESSIVE PART METHOD

❑   If a skill can be broken down into 5 parts, the parts are learned in the following **order**:

◆   learn part 1, learn part 2, perform parts 1 and 2,

◆   learn part 3, perform parts 1,2 and 3,

◆   learn part 4, perform parts 1,2,3 and 4,

◆   learn part 5, perform parts 1,2,3,4 and 5.

◆   **Sequences and routines** are often learned this way.

10.2

TASK COMPLEXITY AND TASK ORGANISATION

A knowledge of **task complexity** and **task organisation** will help the teacher to decide if a skill is best taught in the whole or part method.

Task Complexity :

❑   If a skill is high in complexity it has a large number of parts.

Task Organisation :

❑   This refers to the relationship between the parts of a skill.
❑   Highly organised skills have parts which are closely linked to each other.
❑   Highly organised skills have a large timing component.

If a skill is **high** in **complexity** and **low** in **organisation** then practice in **parts** is recommended.

❑   For example , a single gymnastic move, a gym sequence or trampolining routine.

❑   The whole skill has a large number of parts which are difficult to remember.

❑   It will be easier for the learner if the skill is broken down.

❑   Timing does not play a large part so it does not matter if the skill is broken down.

If a skill is **low** in **complexity** and **high** in **organisation** practice of the **whole** is recommended.

❑   For example , simple jumping, throwing, batting, hitting.

❑   The skill is relatively simple so does not need to be broken down.

❑   Highly organised means that the timing of the skill is paramount.

❑   Timing can only be improved if the skill is practised as a whole.

10.3

Chapter 11 - Practice and Rehearsal

Practice Conditions
Fixed Practice
Variable Practice
Massed v Distributed Practice
Mental Practice or Mental Rehearsal
How Does Mental Rehearsal Work ?
Uses of Mental Rehearsal

Chapter 11 - Practice and Rehearsal

PRACTICE CONDITIONS

Types of Practice would include :

- ❑ **Fixed**
- ❑ **Variable**
- ❑ **Massed**
- ❑ **Distributed**
- ❑ **Mental**

FIXED PRACTICE (set drills)

- ❑ This method is used primarily for **closed skill** practice but can be used to **improve open** skills.
- ❑ The learner practices a set task **without any changes**.
  For example , a gym / trampolining / diving routine, or a set practice or skill in a game (suitable examples could be a free kick in soccer, or service reception in squash).

VARIABLE PRACTICE

- ❑ The learner practices the **same** task in a **number of different ways**.
  For example , for soccer, hockey or basketball, shooting from different angles and distances.
- ❑ This method helps to improve the **schema** of the learner.

MASSED v DISTRIBUTED PRACTICE

- ❑ Should the learner practice **continually** for long spells (**massed**) or should the learner **spread practice out** over the total time available, and hence practice for short periods of time **regularly** (distributed) ?
- ❑ The learner needs to be engaged in a practice method that allows him/her to try hard and concentrate fully. The best method consequently **depends** on the **learner** but as a rule it is agreed that **distributed** practice is most **effective**.

Massed is best :

- ◆ when the performer is **highly motivated** and can cope with long practice sessions.
- ◆ when the task is **simple** and can be fully **learned** in **one session**.
- ◆ in the later stages of learning when the learner can cope with long practice sessions.
- ◆ in the **early stages** of learning when, through **trial and error** the performer is able to stumble across the correct response.

Distributed is best:

- ◆ in the **early stages** of learning when the performer may get easily bored or fatigued.
- ◆ when the **energy demands are high**.
- ◆ when the **task is complex** and will require **a number of practice sessions**.
- ◆ when **motivation is low** or when the task is boring.

MENTAL PRACTICE OR MENTAL REHEARSAL

Definition: **practice or rehearsal of a skill without actual physical movement.**

Used by: skiers, golfers, athletes, tennis players, gymnasts

How: watching a demonstration or film, reading or listening to instructions, imagining movements.

HOW DOES MENTAL REHEARSAL WORK ?

The Neuromuscular Explanation

☐ **Thinking** about movement **actually produces nerve impulses** which fire in the **correct order.**
☐ Consequently mental practice is supposed to result in **actual physical practice**.
☐ There is **little evidence to support this explanation** but it could be helpful in improving the quality of kinaesthetic feedback.

The Cognitive Explanation

☐ **Thinking** about **strategies** and **tactics** can help the performer make the **correct decisions** on the field.
☐ Mental rehearsal is supposed to help the performer **anticipate**.
☐ In this way the performer is better able to **understand** skills and tactics.

The Confidence Explanation

☐ Mental rehearsal has been claimed to improve the **confidence** of performers, which should lead to improved **motivation** and performance.
☐ Mental Rehearsal also **readies** the **performer** for action and stimulates both mental and physical faculties.
☐ It is like a **mental warm up**.

USES OF MENTAL REHEARSAL

☐ Used in a **potentially dangerous** situation as a **safe** way of practising.
☐ Used to improve the **confidence** of performers who have lost or who have low confidence.
☐ Used to help **focus** the mind, as the performer is able to **imagine** a **perfect performance** without harmful distractions.

11.2

Chapter 12 - Teaching Styles

The Mosston Spectrum
The Command Style
The Practice Style
The Reciprocal Style
The Self - Check Style
The Inclusion Style
The Guided Discovery Style
The Problem Solving Style

Chapter 12 - Teaching Styles

TEACHING STYLES

According to **Mosston's** spectrum of teaching styles the way a pupil is taught ranges from the learner being told what to, and how to do it, to, at the other end of the spectrum, the learner solving problems themselves, working out what to do and how to do it.

THE MOSSTON SPECTRUM

- ❑ **Command**
- ❑ **Practice**
- ❑ **Reciprocal**
- ❑ **Self-check**
- ❑ **Inclusion**
- ❑ **Guided discovery**
- ❑ **Problem solving**

THE COMMAND STYLE

- ❑ The **teacher** makes all the **major decisions**.
- ❑ The **learner** is only required to **follow instructions**.
- ❑ The **learner** does **not** make any **decisions**.
- ❑ **Conforming** behaviour is the result, all **learners** should respond in **the same way**.

For example, teaching the forward roll in gymnastics, the teacher's commands would be :
- ◆ starting position,
- ◆ hands flat on the floor,
- ◆ tuck head in,
- ◆ push and kick,
- ◆ rounded back,
- ◆ land on shoulders,
- ◆ push and stand up,
- ◆ finishing position.

Advantages
- ❑ pupils learn skills very **quickly**.
- ❑ ensures **safety** for potentially dangerous skills (for example , the javelin throw).
- ❑ easy for the teacher to gauge the standard of performance as **everyone** is doing the **same task.**

Disadvantages
- ❑ all the **thinking** is taken **away** from the **learner**, so the learner will not know how to react in a new situation.
- ❑ it does **not** fully **stimulate** or **challenge** every pupil.
- ❑ it does **not** cater for **different abilities** within one group.

12.1

THE PRACTICE STYLE

❑   The teacher **sets the task**, the pupils go away and do it.

    For example, in hockey, in a 2 versus 1 practice, the teacher commands would be :
- ◆   draw the defender and pass,
- ◆   do it five times
- ◆   then swap positions.

THE RECIPROCAL STYLE

❑   This involves the **learners working in pairs**.

❑   One is the **doer** the other is the **observer/coach**.

❑   The task is set by the teacher and the points of correct technique/tactics are given to the observer by the teacher.

❑   The **doer practices** the **technique**, the **observer watches** and gives **feedback** related to the information given by the teacher.

Advantages
- ❑   improved **personal** and **social** skills.
- ❑   develops **evaluative** and **performance** skills.
- ❑   learners feel more **in control** of their actions and are liable to be more **motivated**.

Disadvantages
- ❑   the learner may **not** be giving the doer **correct feedback**.

THE SELF - CHECK STYLE

❑   Learners work **individually** on tasks set by the teacher.

❑   The points of **correct technique** are **given** to the learner **by the teacher** (usually on paper to allow for constant checking and rechecking).

❑   The learner **performs** the task and **compares** the **result** with **the ideal performance**.

THE INCLUSION STYLE

❑   This style allows the idea that the **ability range** within a group may be **large**.

❑   Consequently tasks will need to be set which will **stimulate** and challenge **all** pupils, i.e. an easy form of the task for some, hard form of the same task for others.

    For example, in shooting for goal, learners decide at what distance from the goal a shot must be taken : 10m, 20m or 30m.

12.2

THE GUIDED DISCOVERY STYLE

❑   The teacher sets a problem and **leads** the **learner** to the "**correct**" answer.

For example , in cricket, consider the problem of which shot should you play to a short pitched delivery outside leg stump (a ball bouncing high and wide of the stumps).
The teacher is looking for the learner to play the pull or hook shot.
The teacher tries to get the answer by asking :
   ◆ "do you play with a straight or horizontal bat ?
   ◆ " how do you get the power ?
   ◆ " how do you keep the ball down ?"

Advantages
   ❑ the learner develops **an ability to solve problems**.
   ❑ consequently, when faced with a new problem he/she has the ability to solve it.
   ❑ the **learner** should be **fully challenged** and well motivated.
   ❑ the method **stimulates** the learner **mentally** and **physically**.
   ❑ the learner becomes more **independent** and ceases to look to the teacher for answers.
   ❑ the method can lead to **transfer** of learning when the learner discovers similarities between skills and games.

Disadvantages
   ❑ the method can **be time consuming** and slower than command style.
   ❑ the method is **difficult to teach** so that "textbook" performances are arrived at by the learner. Learners attempt to find their own answers, which may be close to "textbook" but not exact.

THE PROBLEM SOLVING STYLE

❑   The **teacher** sets the **problem** and the **learner** finds the **answer**.
❑   Learners are **not** guided towards a "correct" answer but simply **helped** to find an answer.

   For example :
   ◆ in gymnastics the teacher might set the problem for the learner to find a balance on one foot and one hand (he/she would then have to find their own solution to this problem).
   ◆ in basketball, a problem might be to find a way of dribbling past your opponent in a one versus one situation, the learner might find a solution by trial and error.

12.3

Chapter 13 - Guidance

Guidance Methods
Verbal Guidance
Manual Guidance
Visual Guidance

Chapter 13 - Guidance

GUIDANCE METHODS

The **3 methods of communication** a teacher may use are :

- ❑ **Verbal**   the learner is told what to do.

- ❑ **Manual**   the learner's limbs are physically manipulated into the correct position.

- ❑ **Visual**   the learner is shown what to do.

- ❑ Probably **not** all forms of guidance are of **equal significance** to the learner.

- ❑ Some people are **more receptive** to **verbal** guidance, **others to visual**.

- ❑ Different forms of guidance are more or less meaningful at **different stages of learning**.

VERBAL GUIDANCE

- ❑ Verbal guidance can be **from the teacher** or **by the learner to himself/herself.**

- ❑ Verbal instructions should be kept to a **minimum** during the **early** stages of learning due to the learner's **limited capacity** to process information.

- ❑ Instructions should be **brief and to the point**. The teacher should leave a **gap** between the end of **performance** and the **onset of verbal guidance**. This gives the learner **time to process any intrinsic feedback.**

- ❑ **Self verbalisation** can be used to **improve performance**.

- ❑ Verbal guidance is useful at **later stages** of learning when the learner has a **greater capacity** to attend to information.

- ❑ Ultimately the learner must **perform on his/her own**. As learning progresses verbal instruction should be interspersed with greater practice periods.

MANUAL GUIDANCE

Manual guidance can take **2 forms** :

- ❑ If an activity is **potentially hazardous**, **equipment** can be used to prevent the learner making incorrect movements (for example , a somersaulting rig for trampolining).

- ❑ At the **early stage** of learning (especially for the young) the teacher may need to **correctly position** the limbs of the learner (for example , the correct body position for a golf swing).

VISUAL GUIDANCE

- ❑ This method is useful at **every stage of learning** but especially useful for the beginner who needs to gain a **mental picture of correct** performance.

- ❑ **Demonstrations** at the **early stage** of leaning should be at **full speed** to enable the learner to gain an idea of the **correct sequencing or timing** of the movement.

- ❑ At **later stages** of learning demonstrations can be **slowed down** to **highlight points of detail.**

- ❑ Demonstrations must be **perfect** since the learner will be trying to **reproduce** the demonstration.

Sport Psychology - An A level Guide for Teachers and Students

Section 2 - Psychology of Sport

Chapter 14 - Individual Differences - Personality

Chapter 15 - Individual Differences - Attitude

Chapter 16 - Individual Differences - Aggression

Chapter 17 - Individual Differences - Motivation

Chapter 18 - Social Influences - Social Learning

Chapter 19 - Social Influences - Groups and Teams

Chapter 20 - Social Influences - Social Facilitation

Chapter 21 - Social Influences - Leadership

Chapter 22 - Stress

Chapter 14 - Individual Differences - Personality

How are Personalities Formed ?
Trait Theory
Social Learning Theory
Personality Tests
The Minnesota Multiphasic Personality Inventory MMPI
The Eysenck Personality Inventory EPI
Cattell 16 PF Questionnaire
Research Problems
Conceptual Problems
Methodological Problems
Interpretative Problems
Trait Theory
Eysenck's Trait Theory
Eysenck's Personality Dimensions
Cattell's Trait Theory
Trait Theory Assumptions
Trait Theory Limitations
Social Learning Theory
Bandura's Social Learning Theory
Major Concepts in Social Learning Theory
Is there a Sporting Personality ?
Does Personality Determine the Sport we Should Take up ?

Chapter 14 - Individual Differences

PERSONALITY

" The sum total of an **individual's characteristics** which make him/her unique."

❑ Characteristics such as being :

- ◆ **shy**
- ◆ **tense**
- ◆ **relaxed**
- ◆ **sensitive**
- ◆ **aggressive**
- ◆ **outgoing.**

HOW ARE PERSONALITIES FORMED ?

TRAIT THEORY

Trait theories of personality formation state that :

❑ Everyone is **born** with a set of personality characteristics.

❑ The characteristics are arranged in an **hierarchical order** from the strongest to the weakest.

❑ The **situation** does **not** play a major role in explaining behaviour.

SOCIAL LEARNING THEORY

Social Learning theories of personality formation state that :

❑ People behave **differently** in **different situations**.

❑ Personality is **learned**.

❑ Personality is learned through **Observational Learning** and **Modelling** and **Vicarious Conditioning**.

14.1

PERSONALITY TESTS

Personality tests are usually a set of carefully phrased questions which ask the respondent to indicate his/her **answers** which are **influenced** by **personality** or **attitudes**.

THE MINNESOTA MULTIPHASIC PERSONALITY INVENTORY (MMPI)

❑ 550 items or statements which the subject decides are true or false in relation to themselves.

❑ The strength of feeling is found by using a scale.

❑ The **MMPI** was designed to be used by trained psychologists and is not a sport specific test.

(This inventory can be found in full in Fisher A.C. 1978 - see references)

THE EYSENCK PERSONALITY INVENTORY (EPI)

❑ Measures two dimensions, **Neuroticism-Stability** and **Introversion-Extroversion**.

❑ **Neuroticism** refers to general emotional stability and an individual's predisposition to neurotic breakdown under stress.

❑ **Extroversion** refers to uninhibited, outgoing, impulsive and social inclinations of a person.

❑ Each of the two dimensions is measured by a "yes" or "no" response to 24 questions.

(This inventory can be found in Eysenck H. 1968 - see references)

CATTELL 16 PF QUESTIONNAIRE

❑ **16 Primary factors** or primary traits identified by Cattell are measured using a questionnaire.

❑ The questionnaire is in the form of 187 statements to which the subject responds "yes", "occasionally" or "no."

❑ The test gives a score for each of the personality factors.

(This questionnaire can be found in Cattell R.E. and Eber H.W. 1964 - see references)

14.2

RESEARCH PROBLEMS

A large amount of research is contradictory. What reasons are there for the differences in research findings ?

CONCEPTUAL PROBLEMS

❑ Many studies were done without a good reason. Personality studies were often not carefully thought out and designed.

❑ Researchers often used any test they could without knowing why.

❑ Experiments were not rigorous enough.

❑ Ryan (1968) said of some experiments " It isn't surprising that firing into the air at different times and at different places using different ammunition should result in different findings."

METHODOLOGICAL PROBLEMS

❑ Often researchers have tested using inappropriate subjects or only small numbers.

❑ Sometimes they have used inappropriate tests (for example , MMPI, which is a clinical psychiatric test not a sports science test).

INTERPRETIVE PROBLEMS

❑ Many researchers have tried to make too much of findings, they have **overgeneralised** or have **attributed** an **effect** as a **cause**.

For example , volleyball players have been found to be more independent than non volleyball players. Therefore to be a volleyball player a person should be independent. This is not true, effect is being confused with cause.

TRAIT THEORY

❑ According to **trait theorists (Eysenck, Cattell)**:

❑ People **cannot help** the way they act.

❑ Personality is **determined at birth**.

❑ Everyone is born with a **number of personality traits**. A trait is an **underlying** tendency to behave in a certain way.

❑ **Cattell** identified 171 traits. We all have a number of traits in varying degrees of intensity.

❑ Traits are arranged in an **hierarchy** with the strongest at the top and the weakest at the bottom. We are most likely to display our strong traits and less likely to display our weakest traits.

Example of a hierarchical organisation of traits :

 primary trait :   **extrovert**

secondary trait :   **sociability**   **impulsiveness**   **activity**   **liveliness**   **excitability**

❑ Personality does **not change over time** and **situation has little effect** on personality.

EYSENCK'S TRAIT THEORY

According to **Eysenck** the trait that is most likely to be displayed is known as the **personality type. Below** the personality type is a group of strong traits known as **personality traits. Below** weaker traits called **general habits**.

Eysenck ordered personality along **2 dimensions** :
1.   **Introversion - Extroversion**
2.   **Stable - Unstable** (stability)

A person could be a stable extrovert, stable introvert, unstable extrovert, unstable introvert or anywhere in-between.

Later, a **third** dimension was added :
3.   **Psychotic - Non psychotic** (psychotism)

14.4

EYSENCK'S PERSONALITY DIMENSIONS

UNSTABLE

moody   touchy

anxious   restless

rigid   aggressive

sober   excitable

pessimistic   changeable

reserved   impulsive

unsociable   optimistic

quiet   active

INTROVERTED   **EXTROVERTED**

passive   sociable

carefree   outgoing

thoughtful   talkative

peaceful   responsive

controlled   easy going

reliable   lively

even tempered   carefree

calm   leadership

STABLE

❑ According to Eysenck a person could fall anywhere along the two dimensions :

> ❑ **Introverts** are : **passive, quiet and unsociable**.

> ❑ **Extroverts** are : **sociable, outgoing and active**.

> ❑ Emotional **stability** is characterised by being : **calm, even tempered, carefree**

> ❑ Emotional **unstability** is characterised by being : **moody, anxious, rigid.**

> ❑ **Introverts** are more easily **aroused** than **extroverts**.

> ❑ **Introverts** are more likely to **obey rules**.

> ❑ **Introverts** are liable to be **more restrained**.

> ❑ **Introverts** prefer **working alone**, **extroverts** prefer **working in groups**.

14.5

CATTELL'S TRAIT THEORY

Cattell's hierarchy :

- ❑ At the top are **source traits**, behaviours which do not vary and are **most likely** to be displayed. Below are **surface traits** which are groups of behaviour which are displayed with **varying levels of intensity and regularity.**

- ❑ Cattell identified **16 primary traits** and developed **the Cattell 16 PF** questionnaire to measure them.

- ❑ The 16 traits are: **sociability, general ability, ego strength, dominance, surgency, conscientiousness, adventurousness, sensitiveness, pretension, bohemianism, shrewdness, insecurity, radicalism, self-sufficiency, will power, tenseness.**

TRAIT THEORY ASSUMPTIONS

- ❑ Everyone is **born** with a set of **personality characteristics**.

- ❑ The characteristics are arranged in a **hierarchical order from the strongest to the weakest.**

- ❑ The **situation** does **not** play a **major role in explaining behaviour.**

- ❑ To be good at a sport requires a **particular personality**. Top athletes will have similar personalities. **Potential top athletes can be selected at an early age through the use of personality tests.**

TRAIT THEORY LIMITATIONS

According to trait theorists :

- ❑ **Traits** can be **identified**, are **stable** and **enduring**. This has not been proven.

- ❑ Athletes' personality is **different** from that of non athletes. This has not been proven.

- ❑ Certain personality **types** are better **suited** for particular sports. This has not been proven.

- ❑ **Situation** does **not** play a **major role** in personality formation. This has not been proven.

SOCIAL LEARNING THEORY

BANDURA'S SOCIAL LEARNING THEORY

The major theorist was **Bandura**. The main points of the theory are :

❑ People behave **differently** in **different situations**.
❑ Personality is **learned**.
❑ Personality is learned through **Observational Learning** and **Modelling** and **Vicarious Conditioning**.

❑ The main **difference** between trait theory and social learning theory is the importance of the **environment**.

❑ **Social learning theory** states that the **response** to a **stimulus** cannot be **predicted**, people can consciously change their response **depending on the situation**.

For example , if a person is punched, trait theorists would say that a person with high trait aggression would always punch back. Social leaning theorists would argue that the response would depend on the situation (how hard he was hit, by whom, in what environment, what choices he had).

MAJOR CONCEPTS IN SOCIAL LEARNING THEORY

Observational Learning

❑ This is the learning of behaviours simply by **watching** others.
❑ The people who are observed are known as **Models**.
❑ The process is also known as **Modelling**.

For example , a learner tennis player could learn how to play a forehand top spin drive simply by watching a model. He/she could also learn how to respect or abuse the umpire.

Vicarious Conditioning

❑ This is the **learning of emotional responses** through **observational learning**.

For example , if a tennis player gets angry at a call that goes against him/her, the learner could also learn how to become angry and lose his/her cool for no good reason.

14.7

IS THERE A SPORTING PERSONALITY ?

DOES PERSONALITY DETERMINE THE SPORT WE SHOULD TAKE UP ?

Research is inconclusive, but......

❏ Successful athletes display **drive**, **determination**, **leadership** and **self confidence** (Ogilvie).

❏ Successful athletes have a more **positive outlook** (Morgan).

❏ Sports can affect personality. The **demands** of a sport **dictate particular responses**. For example , rugby players need to be aggressive, golfers need to be calm under pressure (Saunders).

❏ Sports people do tend to show traits of **extroversion**, **enthusiasm** and **aggression** (Butt).

❏ People **in team sports** are more **extrovert** than those playing **individual sports** (Davis).

Remember none of this has been fully proven.

Chapter 15 - Individual Differences - Attitude

Attitude
Attitude Formation
The Components of Attitude
Attitude Change
Cognitive Dissonance Theory
Measuring Attitudes
The Cognitive Component
The Affective Component
The Behavioural Component

Chapter 15 - Individual Differences

ATTITUDE

"A learned emotional and behavioural response to a stimulus or situation."

❑ We display attitudes towards **attitude objects**.

❑ The objects can be **places**, **people**, and **concepts** as well as objects.

❑ Examples of **attitude objects** :

- ◆ Maradona
- ◆ Frank Bruno
- ◆ Sally Gunnell
- ◆ Drugs in sport
- ◆ Sporting equipment
- ◆ Wembley stadium

❑ Attitudes can **vary in intensity** from very weak to very strong.

ATTITUDE FORMATION

❑ According to **Triandis**, we **learn** our attitudes either from **direct experience** or from **other people**.

❑ **Direct experience** may be **pleasant** or **unpleasant** and will help us **form an attitude**.

❑ Attitudes are formed through the **agents of socialisation** (parents, teachers and friends). Important people in our lives can help to shape our attitudes. They do it through the use of rewards and punishment, increasing or changing our knowledge, and peer group pressure.

❑ NB **Attitudes do not always predict behaviour**.

❑ Just because a person possesses an opinion it does not necessarily mean they **will** behave in a certain way. Behaviour is often **dependent** on :

- ◆ The **expectations** of **reinforcement** and **punishment**.
- ◆ **Social norms**, the behaviour expected in different groups of people (friends, relatives, work colleagues).

THE COMPONENTS OF ATTITUDE

- ❑ **Cognitive**
- ❑ **Affective**
- ❑ **Behavioural**

The Cognitive Component (information)

- ❑ The **cognitive** component is the **thinking** part of an opinion.
- ❑ It is formed from any **information** a person has about an attitude object.
- ❑ It is what a person **believes** or what they **know** about an attitude object.

The Affective Component (emotion)

- ❑ The **affective** component is the **emotional response** to an attitude object, whether they **like** or **dislike** it.

The Behavioural Component

- ❑ The **behavioural** component is how a person **intends to behave** towards an attitude object.

ATTITUDE CHANGE

- ❑ Attitudes can be changed by **altering** any of the **3 components** of attitude. Attitude change is also explained by **Cognitive Dissonance Theory**.

- ❑ The **cognitive** component can be **changed** by giving a person **new information**. New information will contradict old information and help to change attitude.
  For example , a referee who turned down an appeal for a penalty, may change his opinion if he sees the foul committed on slow motion action replay.

- ❑ The **affective** component can be changed by giving a person **new experiences**. If a person dislikes an attitude object and he/she is placed in a new situation which is enjoyable, then he/she may change his/her attitude.
  For example , a person who is afraid of water is taught to swim in a warm pool with a teacher who gently guides him/her without making him/her frightened.

- ❑ The **behavioural** component can be changed through the use of **reinforcement** and **punishment**. A change in **popularity** of an attitude object may also change the behaviour towards it.
  For example , bicycle helmets are now more popular than ever before, and you don't see many people wearing bicycle clips.

15.2

COGNITIVE DISSONANCE THEORY

❑ If a person holds two ideas that **are in conflict** with each other, this **creates discomfort**.
❑ This **discomfort** is known as **dissonance**.
   For example ,
   ◆ the smoker who is aware of the health hazards,
   ◆ the team manager that wants to play new players but not drop anyone,
   ◆ the player who wants to improve but hates training and therefore often misses it.

❑ The person will want to **reduce the feelings of discomfort**.
❑ This can be achieved by **lessening** the **impact** of one of the **conflicting ideas**.
   For example ,
   ◆ the smoker tries to believe that cancer will not affect her.
   ◆ the team manager tries to believe that the dropped players were getting too old to play in the first team.
   ◆ the player tries to believe that training is not really important.

❑ The teacher should try to **change attitudes** by either :
   ◆ **altering** the **3 components of attitude**
   ◆ or **altering** an idea that is causing **dissonance**.

MEASURING ATTITUDES

❑ By **asking** individuals to record their attitudes on a scale and or **questionnaire**.
❑ By **observing behaviour**.
❑ Using **physiological measurements** such as **heart rate** and **galvanic skin response**.

   The 3 main types of attitude measurement are :
   ◆ **Thurston** Scales
   ◆ **Likert** Scales,
   ◆ **Osgood Semantic Differential** Scales.
      (original references for these 3 scales are found in the references section)

❑ Each of these scales ask for an **emotional** or **physiological** response to an attitude object.
❑ Subjects are asked to record their response using a scale which **identifies a number of possible responses**.

15.3

THE COGNITIVE COMPONENT

❑   The **cognitive component** is to do with **thoughts** and/or **knowledge**.

❑   This is concerned with **how** a person **categorises** his/her **experiences**. We need to determine how a person does this.

Methods :

♦   **Self-rating** of **knowledge** about an attitude object.

♦   **Statistical procedures** to **identify** the **group of stimuli** that an individual associates with an attitude object.

♦   **Associated thoughts** about an attitude object.
Present the subject with a stimulus and ask him/her if he/she associates any of the stimuli with the attitude object.

THE AFFECTIVE COMPONENT

❑   The **affective component** is to do with **emotional responses**.

❑   This is a measure of **likes** and **dislikes** - made both physiologically and emotionally.

Methods :

♦   **Physiological** responses : heart rate, galvanic skin response, palmar sweat measures.

♦   **Verbal scales** (for example **Likert** scales).

An example of a **Likert** scale analysis would be to show a subject an attitude object and ask him/her to ring the appropriate response to the object.

An example question could be about feelings towards a picture, and the response would be given as a choice from :

A	B	C	D	E
very strong	strong	mild	little	none

♦   **Semantic differential**, similar to a Likert scale but easier to administer.

An example **semantic differential** question could be about feelings towards the Olympic Games, and response would be given as a choice from :

good   ....   bad
strong   ....   weak
necessary   ....   unnecessary

15.4

THE BEHAVIOURAL COMPONENT

- ❑ The problem is that **behaviour** is only **partly determined** by **attitude**.
- ❑ To measure the **attitude component**, **other components** (norms, habits, expectations of reinforcements) **have to be controlled.**
- ❑ This is difficult.

Methods :

- ◆ direct **observation** of behaviour

- ◆ use of a **verbal scale**

An example of a verbal scale would be the **Behavioural Differential** which attempts to measure behavioural **intention** towards people.

The type of question asked by this method is explained in an example in which the respondent is asked for his/her attitude to his/her teacher.

The response would be to make choices from :

I would   **I would not**

to each of these statements :

**a) obey this person
b) ask this person for advice
c) invite this person to dinner**

Chapter 16 - Aggression

Aggression
Theories of Aggression
Instinct Theory
Problems with Instinct Theory
Social Learning Theory
Frustration Aggression Theory

Chapter 16 - Individual Differences

AGGRESSION

"A response having for its goal the injury of a human being." **Dolard** (1939)

❑ Aggression must be **directed against** something that is **living** and it must have the intention of **causing** it **pain**.

❑ **Violence** is a severe form of aggression.

❑ **Instrumental aggression** is aggression occurring in the **achievement of a non aggressive goal**.
   For example , in boxing, or in attacking the other team's best player in order to have more chance of winning.

❑ **Reactive aggression** is the aggressive **response** to **other aggressive behaviour**.
   For example , getting involved in football hooliganism.

❑ **Instrumental aggression** is a **means** to an **end**, the end being **winning**. **Reactive aggression** has only **one end**, namely **harming an opponent**.

❑ **Assertion** is slightly **different** from **aggression**.

❑ **Assertion is a form of instrumental aggression**, aggressive behaviour that is controlled and within the rules.

16.1

THEORIES OF AGGRESSION

❑   **Instinct theory**   **aggression is innate**
❑   **Social Learning theory**   **aggression is learned**
❑   **Frustration theory**   **aggression results from frustration**

INSTINCT THEORY

❑   Instinct Theory asserts that **aggression is innate**. We are all **born** with a certain **predisposition to be aggressive.**

❑   Aggressive tendencies are **difficult to control**.

❑   According to "rainbutt" theory, the stress of everyday life **builds up the aggression** inside us. **Eventually** the aggression will be let out, often **in a big outburst of aggression**.

❑   Sport acts as **cathartic release**, purging all aggressive tendencies.
     Instinct theorists see **aggression in sport as being healthy**. Within sport aggression is **controlled**. If sport was not available aggression would be let out in more **dangerous** ways.

PROBLEMS WITH INSTINCT THEORY

❑   The theory has **not been proven**.

❑   It does **not** consider the importance of the **environment** and **situational factors**.

❑   It assumes sport **allows** people to be **aggressive**. The rules make it difficult to be aggressive.

❑   It assumes that **playing sport can lead to a more peaceful society**. Some of the largest sporting nations are also the same nations that are waging war.

16.2

SOCIAL LEARNING THEORY

- ❑ **Social Learning Theory** asserts that aggression is **learned**.

- ❑ Aggression is learned through the **primary socialising agents**, parents, teachers and friends.

- ❑ A person can **learn** an aggressive act either by being **taught** or **through observational learning and modelling.**

- ❑ **Sport** can promote both **aggressive** and **non-aggressive** acts.

  - ◆ If a learner observes a role model perform an aggressive act he/she will want to copy it.
  - ◆ If a learner observes a role model perform a non-aggressive act he/she will want to copy it.
  - ◆ If a learner is rewarded for an aggressive act he/she will want to repeat it.
  - ◆ If a learner is rewarded for a non-aggressive act he/she will want to repeat it.
  - ◆ If a learner is punished for an aggressive act he/she is likely not to repeat it.

- ❑ **Sport** can be used to **teach** aggressive or non-aggressive acts depending on how **rewards** and **punishments** are used.

- ❑ When used effectively, sport is seen as a very valuable way of **teaching the attitudes valued by society**. Such attitudes would include : fair play, cooperation, how to cope with defeat and victory, and how to be assertive without being aggressive.

FRUSTRATION AGGRESSION THEORY

- ❑ This is the most widely held theory.

- ❑ Aggression is the **result of frustrating circumstances**. If people are unable to achieve a goal they respond aggressively.

- ❑ Sport is frustrating as one player (or team) is always trying to prevent the other from winning. As a consequence it is **sport** itself that **can cause aggression**.

- ❑ This theory does **not** explain why **people are not aggressive** when the **situation** is frustrating.

- ❑ **Teachers** should therefore **help performers** cope **with frustrating circumstances** by **rewarding non-aggressive** acts and **punishing aggressive** acts.

16.3

Chapter 17 - Individual Differences - Motivation

Motivation
Types of Motivation
Measuring Motivation
Tutko and Richards Motivational Rating Scale
Kenyon Attitude towards Physical Activity Inventory
Alderman and Wood Incentive Motivation Inventory
Optimum Motivation
Hull's Drive theory
The Inverted U or Yerkes Dodson Law
Optimum Levels of Arousal
Achievement Motivation
The Personality Factors
The Situational Factors
The Combination of Personality and Situational Factors
Implications for the Coach
Attribution Theory
The Model
Attribution Theory - the Main Points
How can we Use Attribution Theory and Achievement Motivation ?
Bandura's Self Efficacy Theory

Chapter 17 - Individual Differences

MOTIVATION

Stallings (1966) "An internal factor that arouses and directs behaviour".

❏ **Motivation** is the **power** or **drive** behind why we do something.

❏ **Motivation** is responsible for : the **selection** and **preference** for an **activity**, the **persistence** at the activity, the **intensity** and **effort** put into performance.

TYPES OF MOTIVATION

Intrinsic Motivation

❏ This derives from feelings from **inside ourselves**, for example, fun, enjoyment, joy, satisfaction.

Extrinsic Motivation

❏ This derives from feelings coming from gaining **external rewards** both **physical** (money, trophies) and **emotional** (praise).

Primary and Secondary Motivation

❏ **Primary motivation** is derived from the **activity itself**.
❏ **Secondary motivation** comes from **anything other** than taking part.
   For example , an activity undertaken to please a coach or friends, or to gain medals.

Positive and Negative Motivation

❏ **Any aspect** of competing can have a positive or negative effect on motivation.
❏ **Winning** is **positively** motivating, **losing** can be **negatively** motivating.
❏ The **audience** can have both a positive and negative effect.

MEASURING MOTIVATION

The following researchers have developed scales / inventories which attempt to put a numerical measure on this concept.

TUTKO AND RICHARDS (1972) MOTIVATIONAL RATING SCALE

This scale identifies 11 traits which contributed to highly motivated athletes :

Aggression	**Determination**
Coachability	**Leadership**
Emotional Control	**Responsibility**
Mental Toughness	**Trust**
Drive	**Conscientiousness**
Self confidence	

(An example of this scale can be found in Corbin C. 1978 - see references)

KENYON (1968) ATTITUDE TOWARDS PHYSICAL ACTIVITY INVENTORY

This inventory identifies and attempts to measure 6 reasons why sportspeople take part in physical activity :

Social	**Aesthetic**
Heath and Fitness	**Acetic**
Vertigo	**Chance**

(The original work on this inventory can be found in Kenyon G.S. 1968 - see references)

Appendix 2 - outlines an example of an **Attitude to Physical Activity Questionnaire**
- this is suitable for an analysis of student motivation.

ALDERMAN AND WOOD (1976) INCENTIVE MOTIVATION INVENTORY

This inventory identifies and attempts to measure 7 reasons why sportspeople take part in physical activity :

Affiliation	**Power**
Aggression	**Stress**
Excellence	**Success**
Independence	

(This inventory can be found in Alderman R.B. 1970 - see references)

OPTIMUM MOTIVATION

❑ The coach will need to manipulate the athlete's level of motivation in order to **maximise** performance.

❑ The relationship between **motivation** and **performance** is very **similar** to the relationship between **arousal** and **performance**, the performer who is highly motivated will also be aroused.

The relationship between arousal and performance has been explained **by two theories** :

HULL'S DRIVE THEORY

❑ This theory explains why, for a lot of **beginners**, it is **easy** to perform a skill when there is **no pressure**, but when **pressure is introduced** the beginner starts to make **mistakes**.

❑ Alternatively an **increase in pressure** can actually **help** the **skilled athlete** perform to the **best** of his/her ability.

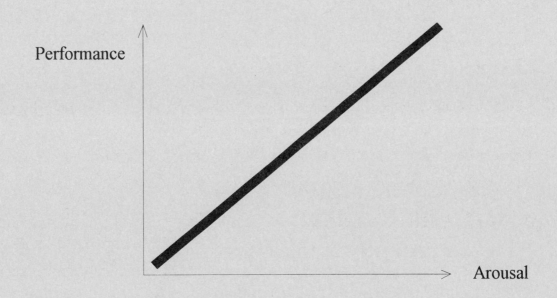

❑ Drive Theory states that **performance increases with increasing levels of arousal**, therefore the more arousal the better the performance.

❑ But there are exceptions !

17.3

Hull's Drive theory states that :
Performance = Habit x Drive

❑ **Habit** refers to the **strength** of the learned response or skill, or whether the correct response has been **practised** until it has become **habitualised**. Any response can have a **strong or weak habit** depending on **the level of practice at that skill.**

❑ **Drive** refers to **the level of arousal** of the performer.

❑ **Increased** levels of **arousal** are said to bring about the **dominant response** (strongest from a number of possibilities).

❑ While **learning** (the activity or skill), the **dominant response** is usually **incorrect** (low level of habit).

❑ When the skill has been fully **learned**, the **dominant response** is usually **correct** (high level of habit).

❑ **Until a skill has been well learned**, any **increase** in **arousal** will probably result in an **decrease** in **performance**.

❑ Once a skill is **fully learned, an increase in arousal** is more likely to bring about an **increase in performance**

THE INVERTED U OR YERKES DODSON LAW

❑ This theory asserts that performance **increases with arousal** up to a **point** where increased levels of arousal bring about **decreased levels of performance**.

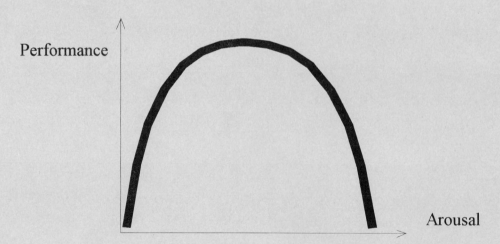

❑ A **certain level** of **arousal** is obviously needed to **perform well. Too much arousal** can make the performer **tense, overanxious** and **liable** to make **mistakes**. The main aim for the performer is to reach the **optimum level of arousal**.

17.4

OPTIMUM LEVELS OF AROUSAL

The optimum level of arousal is dependent on a number of factors including **task difficulty, level of learning** and **individual differences**.

❑ For **simple skills**, the learner will need to be **more aroused** than for **complex skills**.

❑ If the task is **simple**, it is easy for the performer to become **disinterested**. Higher levels of **arousal** will ensure **greater concentration**.

❑ **Complex skills** require large amounts of **attentional capacity** and so need **lower** levels of **arousal**. **Excessive arousal** can cause **frustration** and **narrowing** of **attentional focus** (tunnel vision). This can be detrimental to performance.

❑ **High levels of arousal** for **fine motor skills** such as snooker can be **detrimental to performance**, due to unwanted increases in muscle tension.

❑ **Gross motor skills** such as weight lifting, need relatively **higher levels of arousal** than fine motor skills.

❑ **Hazardous** activities will require **high levels of arousal**.

❑ At the **early stages** of learning, **arousal levels** need to be relatively **low**. Too much arousal can affect the learners ability to attend to information.

❑ At **later stages** of learning when the learner has **spare attentional capacity**, **greater levels** of **arousal** can help motivate the performer.

❑ **Personality** can affect **optimum arousal levels**. The **introvert** may find it easy to become **over aroused**, whilst the **extrovert** will need **increased** levels of **arousal** to reach the **optimum** point.

ACHIEVEMENT MOTIVATION

According to **Atkinson**, whenever a person is faced with a task, the decision to accept or reject the task is based on both **personality** and **situational** factors.

THE PERSONALITY FACTORS

❑   the **motive** to **succeed** (**Ms**) - whose purpose would be to gain pride or satisfaction.
❑   the **motive** to **avoid failure** (**Maf**) - whose purpose would be to avoid shame or humiliation.

◆   In any challenging situation everyone, will have both **Ms** and **Maf**. Whichever feeling is strongest will determine whether the task is accepted or rejected

◆   High achievers have high **Ms** and low **Maf**. They would concentrate on success and not worry about failure.

◆   Low achievers have low **Ms** and high **Maf**. They would worry about how they would feel if they fail.

Some texts now use the terms **Nach** and **Naf** to replace **Ms** and **Maf**, where **Nach** is the **need** to **achieve**, and **Naf** is the **need** to **avoid failure**.

THE SITUATIONAL FACTORS

❑   the **incentive** value of **success** (**Is**) and the **incentive** value of **failure** (**If**)
❑   the **probability** of **success** (**Ps**) and the **probability** of **failure** (**Pf**)

◆   The **incentive value** refers to how much the individual thinks he/she would **gain** or **lose** by accepting the task.

◆   **Is** is inversely proportional to **Ps**. In other words as **Ps** increases **Is** reduces.
    For example, the **Ps** for a hole in one at golf is very small - so the **Is** is huge.

THE COMBINATION OF PERSONALITY AND SITUATIONAL FACTORS

The personality factors combined with the situational factors result in a person having :

❑   the **tendency** to approach **success** (**Ts**)   **Ts**   = **Ms x Ps x Is**

❑   the **tendency** to **avoid failure** (**Taf**)   **Taf**   = **Maf x Pf x If**

❑   Whichever of the two tendencies is **strongest** will determine whether a task is **accepted** or **rejected**.

17.6

IMPLICATIONS FOR THE COACH

A coach wants an athlete with a **high tendency** to **approach success** and a low tendency to avoid failure.

What can the coach do to improve **Ts** and reduce **Taf** ?

- ◆ Manipulate the personality factors by improving **Ms** and reducing **Maf**.
- ◆ Manipulate the **situational** factors.

❑ **Increase Ms** by increasing the amount of **positive reinforcement**, thus increasing the feelings of **pride** and **satisfaction** associated with success.

❑ **Reduce Maf** by **reducing punishment** hence lowering the chances of the performer worrying about failure, thus reducing the negative feelings associated with failure.

❑ **Reduce Maf** by **focusing negative feedback** on **effort** rather than ability. The performer will then know that he/she can do better next time. This will reduce the chance of "**learned helplessness**."

❑ Any task set should have a **choice of difficulty** so that **everyone can achieve**. If a single task is set, those with high **Maf** may not want to try.

❑ Encourage the low achiever to become familiar with success by placing them in situations where **success is guaranteed**, then gradually **increase the task difficulty**. Any failures should be attributed to lack of effort rather than ability.

❑ Try **not** to place the performer into situations where **defeat is inevitable**. If this is unavoidable, alter the criteria for success.
For example, in a badminton match, success could be measured by not losing by more than five points in each game.

❑ To sustain motivation in those performers with high **Ms**, tasks set should be **challenging**.

❑ Achieve the **correct** level of **Ps** to ensure adequate motivation. If the task were too easy it could be perceived as boring , too hard and it may be impossible to achieve.

❑ Achieve the **correct** level of **Is**, too little and the task could be perceived as pointless.

Appendix 3 sets out a questionnaire suitable for students, which would assess achievement motivation

ATTRIBUTION THEORY

❏   Developed by **Weiner (1974), attribution theory** is concerned with the **reasons** (**attributions**) performers give to their success or failure.

❏   **Weiner** suggested that the reason that high achievers and low achievers became so, was a **difference** in their **attributions** for **success** and **failure**.

❏   **Weiner's 4 Attributions** are :
- ◆   **Ability**
- ◆   **Effort**
- ◆   **Luck**
- ◆   **Task Difficulty**

❏   The 4 attributions can be placed along 2 dimensions :
- ◆   **Locus of Causality**
- ◆   **Stability**

❏   More recently a third dimension has been identified namely **Controllability**.

THE MODEL

		Locus of Causality	
		INTERNAL	**EXTERNAL**
Stability	**STABLE**	Ability	Task Difficulty
	UNSTABLE	Effort	Luck

❏   **Locus of Causality** refers to whether the performance **outcome** could be as a **result** of factors under the **control of the performer** (the internal factors of effort and ability), or as a **result** of factors **beyond the control of the performer** (the external factors of task difficulty and luck).

❏   **Stability** refers to whether the performance **outcome** is **fixed** and **unchanging** or can **vary over time**.

❏   **Ability** and **task difficulty** are **stable** and **fixed** during the period of performance. **Effort** and **luck** may **change** from **performance to performance** or **within** the performance.

ATTRIBUTION THEORY - THE MAIN POINTS

❏   Often individuals make **internal attributions** for **success** and **external attributions** for **failure**. We like to feel that we are responsible for success but that failure was due to factors beyond our control.

❏   The **stability** dimension is usually seen to be **related** to **future expectations**. If we attribute success or failure to stable factors then next time we compete we will expect the same result.

❏   High and Low achievers attribute success and failure to different factors.

❏   **High achievers** tend to attribute **success** to **internal** factors and **failure** to **unstable** factors.

❏   **Low achievers** tend to attribute **success** to **external** factors and **failure** to **stable** factors.

❏   **Girls** tend to have **attributions** consistent with those of **low achievers**. **Boys** tend to have higher **expectations** of **success**.

Appendix 4 sets out a student questionnaire which looks for attribution to a success and a failure situation. Groups such as male / female or high / low sport achievers can be compared.

HOW CAN WE USE ATTRIBUTION THEORY ACHEIVEMENT MOTIVATION ?

The coach should try to make the performer :

❑   Attribute **success** to **internal** factors in order to maximise confidence and satisfaction.

❑   Attribute **success** to **stable** factors in order to maximise the expectation of future success.

❑   Attribute **failure** to **external** factors in order to minimise negative feelings.

❑   Attribute failure to **unstable** factors in order to minimise the expectations of future losses. Be careful when attributing failure to lack of effort if the performer has tried his/her hardest.

❑   Redefine success where **ability** is the **reason** for **failure**.

❑   The process by which attributions are changed is known as **attribution retraining**.

   ◆   In order to change to a high achieving status, low achievers will need to learn how to attribute success and failure to the same reasons given by high achievers.

❑   Low achievers often suffer from "**Learned Helplessness**."

   ◆   **Learned helplessness** is the acquired belief that one has **no control** over negative events, that **failure is inevitable**.
   ◆   Performers with learned helplessness will need **attribution retraining**.
   ◆   Their **confidence** levels will need to be **increased** along with a belief that they **can control their own destiny.**

❑   Low achievers will need attribution retraining.

❑   High achievers often have high levels of "**self efficacy**".

   ◆   **Self efficacy** is a **situational** form of **self confidence**.
   ◆   Studies have suggested that when all else is equal the performer with highest self efficacy will win.
   ◆   Coaches should try to **encourage self efficacy**.

BANDURA'S SELF EFFICACY THEORY

Gould (1981) "**self efficacy** is a **situation specific** form of **self confidence**."

❑ **Bandura** states that **self efficacy** predicts **actual performance** when skill and motivation is present.

❑ If you are as motivated and skilful as your opponent whoever has the highest self efficacy will win.

❑ According to Bandura self efficacy can be improved following his **4 component model**.

Self Efficacy component	How to Improve Self Efficacy
◆ **Performance accomplishments**	Highlight past performances. This has the most powerful effect on self efficacy.
◆ **Vicarious experiences**	Show the performer a demonstration of the required performance. This will persuade the performer that the task is achievable.
◆ **Verbal persuasion**	Verbally encourage the performer. Tell him/her that he/she has the ability to succeed.
◆ **Emotional arousal**	Get the performer to feel confident about his/her level of arousal, and then to alter the level of arousal to achieve the optimum level.

17.11

Chapter 18 - Social Influences - Social Learning

Social Learning
Social Learning Theory
Bandura's Model of Observational Learning

Chapter 18 - Social Influences

SOCIAL LEARNING

❑   This section looks at the effects that **people** can have on **behaviour** and **performance**.

❑   According to **social learning theory (SLT)** all **behaviour** is **learned**. The greatest amount of learning takes place at an early age through socialisation.

❑   **Socialisation** is the process by which **society trains its children** to behave like adults.

❑   Through **socialisation** we learn :

  ◆   The correct patterns of behaviour (**norms**).
  ◆   What is right and wrong (**values**).
  ◆   Our **status** and **role** in society.

❑   **Physical Education and sport** can act as **part** of the **socialisation** process. It helps to transmit the norms and values of society. Sport is seen as developing values such as **fair play, tolerance, cooperation, teamwork and determination.**

❑   According to **SLT** we learn what our behaviour should be through the processes of **observational learning** and **modelling.**

18.1

SOCIAL LEARNING THEORY (BANDURA 1969)

Observational Learning :   People can learn merely by observing the behaviour of others.

Modelling :   A person can learn behaviours by observing a model perform.
                    For modelling to work the model's performance must be correct.

BANDURA'S MODEL OF OBSERVATIONAL LEARNING

❑   **Learning** takes place because the **observer is able to correct sensory images** and **arrange them in time order** (temporally) so that they make sense.

The model has **4 stages** :

❑   **Attention Processes** , which refers to **what to look for** in the model's performance.

◆   To improve observational learning, the learner will need to use **selective attention** to pick out the **relevant** cues. This is because he/she will have **limited attentional capacity**. A teacher will need to highlight the relevant cues.

❑   **Retention Processes** , which refers to **how to remember** the model's performance.

◆   To improve observational learning, retention will be helped by **repeated demonstrations** and **mental rehearsal**.

❑   **Motor Reproduction** , which refers to **how to copy** the model's performance.

◆   To improve observational learning, the learner's performance can be improved with **practice**, and through the use of both **intrinsic** and **extrinsic feedback**.

❑   **Motivational Processes** , which refers to **the reasons why** one would copy the model's performance.

◆   To improve observational learning, the learner must first **want** to copy the model's performance, he/she must have a **reason**. The **status** of the model can affect motivation. The **importance of the task** will also affect motivation.

Chapter 19 - Social Influences - Groups and Teams

Groups and Teams
Groups
Steiner's Model of Group Performance
The Ringlemann Effect and Social Loafing
Other Ways of Improving Group Success

Chapter 19 - Social Influences

GROUPS AND TEAMS

GROUPS

According to **Carron** (1980), a group has the following characteristics :

- ❑ **a collective identity**
- ❑ **a sense of shared purpose**
- ❑ **structured patterns of communication**

❑ A successful team is one which **maximises** these characteristics.

❑ A successful team has good **cohesion**. Cohesion is the **motivation** that keeps group members **together** and which **resists** the group **breaking up.** Group members may be motivated to be in the group because of the **success** it brings them or because they value the **relationships** within the group.

❑ A **coach** must use a **knowledge** of **groups** and **group dynamics** to make the team function more effectively.

STEINER'S MODEL OF GROUP PERFORMANCE

According to **Steiner**:
    Actual group performance = potential productivity - losses due to faulty processes

❑ **Potential productivity** = the group's best performance given its resources (skill, knowledge).

❑ **Faulty processes** = things that can go wrong for reasons of **co-ordination losses** and **motivation losses**.

❑ **Co-ordination losses** are due to the team not working effectively together (for example through poor timing or strategy).

❑ **Motivation losses** are due to the team members losing the will to do their best.

❑ The coach will need to put together a group with high potential productivity whilst trying to minimise losses due to faulty process. **Minimising losses** could be achieved by :
- ◆ **Organising practices** so that all team members are certain of their role.
- ◆ **Overlearning** set plays in order to get the timing right.
- ◆ **Manipulating** the use of **rewards** to optimise **motivation** levels.

❑ Coaches should not just pick the best players for a team, but those who are most likely to **get on with each other.**

19.1

THE RINGLEMANN EFFECT AND SOCIAL LOAFING

❑ According to **Ringlemann**, individual performance **decreases** with an increase in group size. From studies into tug-of-war it was found that an eight did not pull eight times harder than eight solo pullers.

❑ According to **Latane** (1979), **social loafing** is said to occur when an individual suffers motivational losses within a group. The individual feels that a reduction in effort would not be noticed. They can **hide** within the group and take it easy.

❑ A coach will need to **avoid** social loafing. This can be done by :

♦ Trying to make certain that team members' **contributions** are **valued**.
♦ **Highlighting individual performance** (an example would be by using statistics in basketball - shooting, rebounding and assists).
♦ **Positively reinforcing** good team and individual performances.
♦ **Fostering team spirit**, if each team member feels they are part of the team, social loafing can be reduced.
♦ **Assigning individual roles** and **responsibilities**.
♦ Heightening the **importance** of **units** within teams (for example the defensive unit in hockey).
♦ Making players who are loafing **aware** of it (talk to them or even substitute them in a game).
♦ Increasing the **social support** given by other team members.

OTHER WAYS OF IMPROVING GROUP SUCCESS

❑ Ensure team members know their responsibilities.

❑ Provide opportunities to **socialise**.

❑ Ensure team members **contributions** are **valued** and **rewarded**.

❑ Share **ownership** of **ideas**. Discussion is more likely to bring **consensus**. Team members will work harder if ideas are not imposed.

❑ Emphasise **group goals.**

Chapter 20 - Social Influences - Social Facilitation

Social Facilitation

Chapter 20 - Social Influences

SOCIAL FACILITATION

Zajonc (1965) "The consequences upon behaviour which derive from the sheer presence of others."

❑   The term **others** may mean **other performers** or an **audience**.

❑   The **audience** may be **silent** or **noisy**.

❑   The name given to fellow performers is "**coactors**."

❑   The effect of others is to **increase arousal.**

❑   The effect of arousal on performance is described by the curve of the "**Inverted U**."

❑   Thus **increase** in arousal can have a **positive** or **negative** effect on performance.

❑   Performance effects will be **positive** if the **task** is **well learned** (increase in performance).

❑   Performance effects will be **negative** if the task is **not fully learned** (decrease in performance).

❑   According to **Cottrell** (1965), the effect that others have on performance is dependent on whether **the performer perceives** the others as **evaluating** his or her **performance**. A subsequent **rise in arousal** levels was said to result from **evaluation apprehension**.

❑   The **effect** the **audience** has on **performance** depends on a number of factors :

◆   **Size of audience**   Larger crowds will increase arousal.

◆   **Proximity to the performers**   The closer the audience the larger the increase in arousal.

◆   **Intentions of the audience**   This can cause a positive or negative effect depending on the personality of the performer.

◆   **Level of learning of the task**   Performance will generally increase if the task is well learned, and will decrease if the task is not fully learned.

◆   **Personality of the performer**   Extroverts perform better when aroused, introverts can easily be over aroused.

◆   **Type of task**   Gross motor skills benefit from increased arousal levels, fine motor skills need low levels of arousal.

Chapter 21 - Social Influences - Leadership

Leadership
Leadership Types
Leadership Models
Chelladurai's Multidimensional Model
Feidler's Contingency Model

Chapter 21 - Social Influences

LEADERSHIP

Barrow (1977) "The process of influencing individuals and groups towards set goals."

❏   According to **Trait** theorists leaders are **born**.
❏   According to **Social Learning** theorists leaders are **bred** - formed throughout life by **social** or **environmental influences**.

LEADERSHIP TYPES

Authoritarian   **Democratic**   **Laissez-faire**

Strict ━━━━━━━━━━━━━━━━━━━━▶ **Relaxed**

❏   The **Authoritarian** leader **makes** all the **decisions**, the **democratic** leader **shares** the **decision** making, and the **laissez-faire** leader **sits back** and lets **others** make **decisions**. Each type can be effective in different situations.

21.1

LEADERSHIP MODELS

CHELLADURAI'S MULTIDIMENSIONAL MODEL

❑   According to Chelladurai there are five types of leadership behaviour :

      1 Training and Instruction   (behaviour aimed at improving performance)
      2 Democratic   (allows decisions to be made collectively)
      3 Autocratic   (personal authority)
      4 Social support   (concern for the well being of others)
      5 Rewarding   (positive reinforcement)

❑   These behaviours can be measured using the **Leadership Scale for Sport (LSS)**.

The original reference for this scale is in Chelladurai P. 1978 - see references. **Appendix 5** sets out a student version of the **LSS**.

❑   A good leader will need to **demonstrate all five types** of behaviour.

❑   The leader's **behaviour** is only one factor that controls a person's ability to lead.

❑   Chelladurai states there are **three factors** that control a person's ability to lead :

    ♦   **Situation characteristics**
        environmental conditions such as whether the leader leads individuals or groups, the time the group has spent together, the type of task.

    ♦   **Leader characteristics**
        the type of leader (autocratic, democratic).

    ♦   **Member characteristics**
        the players preferred leadership style and their expectations.

❑   The leader will be most effective when these three factors are **compatible**.
   For example :
    ♦   when the **situation** calls for a leader to take charge,
    ♦   when the **leader's** style is **autocratic**, and
    ♦   when the **members prefer** their leader to be **autocratic**.

FIEDLER'S CONTINGENCY MODEL

❏ According to **Fiedler**, the **effectiveness** of a leader is dependent on 2 factors :
   ◆ **the personality of the coach**
   ◆ **the situation.**

❏ The personality of the leader is measured using the **Least Preferred Co-worker Scale (LPC)**. The test records whether a leader is **task orientated** (concerned with achievement) or **person orientated** (concerned with the members of the group).

   The **LPC** can be found in Fiedler F. 1967 - see references.
   Appendix 6 sets out a student version of the **LPC**.

❏ The **type of situation** is said to determine which type of leader will be most successful.

❏ According to **Fiedler** :

   ◆ A **task orientated leader** is most successful in the most favourable and least favourable situations.

   ◆ A **person orientated leader** is most successful in moderately favourable situations.

   ◆ The **situation** is said to be most **favourable** when **relationships are warm**, the **task** has a **clear structure** and the **leader** is **powerful**.

Chapter 22 - Stress

The Nature of Stress
Arousal
Anxiety
Stress
The Measurement of Anxiety or Stress
Self Report Questionnaires
Physiological Measures
Behavioural Measures
The Management of Stress
Mental Preparation for Performance
Mental Rehearsal
Goal Setting

Chapter 22 - Stress

THE NATURE OF STRESS

Stress :   A stimulus resulting in arousal or a response to a situation.

Arousal :   The state of activation or excitement a person has in any situation.

Anxiety :   A reaction to stress resulting in over arousal.

AROUSAL

❏   The relationship between arousal and performance.

The Inverted "U" Theory :

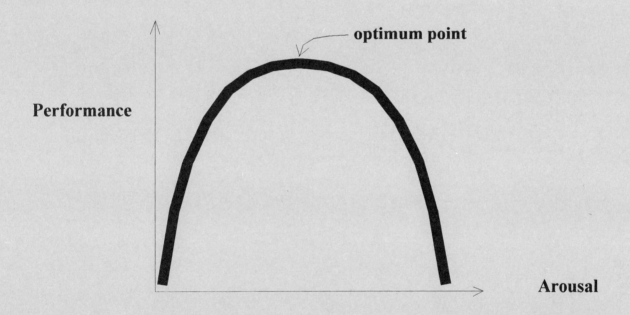

❏   **Performance increases** with **increasing** levels of **arousal** up to a point (**the optimum point**). **After** this point **increasing** levels of arousal bring about **decreasing** levels of performance.

❏   The **optimum point** relates to the most beneficial level of motivation for any task. It can change depending on the **task**, **level of learning** and **personality** of the performer. For a more detailed explanation see the section on Arousal.

❏   The **coach** will try to get the athlete to the **optimum** point, **motivate** the athlete but **not over motivate**.

Drive Theory :

An alternative to the Inverted "U" theory is Drive Theory.

❑ First developed by **Hull** in 1943, **Drive Theory** states that performance **increases** with **increasing** levels of **arousal**, so the more arousal (and hence motivation) the better the performance.

❑ However Hull added that this would only be the case if the **skill had previously been well learned**.

❑ Performance levels for a highly motivated beginner would probably reduce.

ANXIETY

Anxiety is a **physiological** and **emotional** response to **stress**.

Emotional Feelings	**Physiological Signs**
alert, awake, scared, apprehensive, negative thoughts	increased muscle tension, high respiration rate, high heart rate, increased perspiration, relaxation of smooth muscle.

❑ Anxiety results in **over arousal**.

❑ Anxiety levels can **vary over time** and can **vary in intensity**.

State anxiety :   a person's immediate emotional state in any one situation.

Trait anxiety :   a person's inbuilt proneness to anxiety, his/her general arousal level.

❑ Anxiety is a **response** to stress. **Stress** is perceived as **threatening** and results in the body being made ready for the **Fight or Flight response**. The threat can either be the threat of injury or ego threat.

STRESS

- ❑ The word **stress** has often been used to mean **anxiety**.
- ❑ More recently its meaning has slightly **altered**.
- ❑ Anxiety is **over arousal** which results in a **decrease in performance**.
- ❑ **Stress** is combined in the **circumstances** that lead a person to become **anxious**.
- ❑ **Stress** can be both **beneficial** or **harmful**.

- ❑ **Stressors** are **environmental conditions** that cause stress.
- ❑ Examples of **stressors** are:

  ### Competition
  Competition naturally increases arousal levels and causes stress

  ### Frustration
  Being prevented from achieving a goal

  ### Climate
  Both hot and cold climates can be stressful

Stress as a Beneficial Agent :

- ❑ Stress can be **beneficial** because it energises the performer into trying their hardest.
- ❑ Some people seek out **stressful experiences** because of the **extreme feelings** that can be gained. These feelings are known as **eustress**.
- ❑ They are the feelings looked for by those participating in hazardous activities like parachuting and bungy jumping.

Stress as a Negative Agent :

- ❑ Stress can be **negative** when the performer becomes **overaroused**.
- ❑ The performer then becomes **tense** and **anxious**, he/she suffers a loss in concentration and is more likely to make a mistake.

THE MEASUREMENT OF ANXIETY OR STRESS

SELF REPORT QUESTIONNAIRES

❑ These are simple to administer but subjects may lie !

❑ **Marten's Sport Competitive Anxiety Test (SCAT)**
Measures the emotional and physiological responses to stress in the **competitive environment**.

The full details of this test can be found in Martens R. 1977 - see references. **Appendix 7** sets out a version of this suitable for use by students.

❑ **Speilberger's State, Trait Anxiety Inventory (STAI)**
Measures the emotional and physiological responses to stress in **general**, and in **specific situations**.

The full details of this inventory can be found in Speilberger C. 1977 - see references. **Appendix 8** sets out a version of this suitable for use by students.

PHYSIOLOGICAL MEASURES

❑ These produce reliable results but are expensive to administer.

❑ **The Galvanic Skin Response** :   measures skin conductivity.

❑ **Sudorimeter** :   measures sweating.

❑ **Electrocardiogram (ECG)** :   measures heart rate.

❑ **Electromyogram (EMG)** :   measures muscle tension.

❑ **Electroencephalogram (EEG)** :   measures brain wave activity

BEHAVIOURAL MEASURES

❑ Involve **observing** the performance of sports players.
❑ This method is very **subjective**.

22.4

THE MANAGEMENT OF STRESS

Educational Techniques

❑ **Educational** techniques get the performer to **understand** anxiety, and the level of stress they need in order to perform well.

❑ The performer will be **taught** how to "psyche" themselves up and calm themselves down.

Cognitive Techniques

❑ Cognitive techniques help the performer to **reduce worry** and **negative thoughts** by thinking about the task.

♦ **Thought stopping**   When the performer feels a negative thought he/she should immediately think "STOP" and substitute a positive thought.

♦ **Imagery**   The performer imagines him/herself in a calm peaceful setting where he/she is in control.

♦ **Directing attention**   The performer directs his/her attention to particular aspects of performance thereby avoiding negative thought.

Relaxation Techniques

♦ **Slow deep breathing**   Can help to reduce respiration rate and heart rate.

♦ **Progressive relaxation**   (Due to Jacobson 1938) This involves the tensing and then relaxing of various muscle groups. The effect is to super-relax the muscles.

♦ **Meditation**   Can relax the mind. It is assumed that a relaxed mind will help to relax the body.

♦ **Biofeedback**   Gives the performer immediate physiological feedback (for example by monitoring heart and respiration rate). The performer then tries to reduce any of the aspects being measured. He/she will receive immediate feedback relating to the success of his/her efforts.

22.5

MENTAL PREPARATION FOR PERFORMANCE

MENTAL REHEARSAL

❑ Imagery can be used to reduce anxiety by **visualising relaxing situations**.

❑ Imagery can be used as a form of **practice**. Mental rehearsal can take two forms :

♦ **Internal** - imagining how the movement felt.

♦ **External** - imagining the sporting environment.

How Can Mental Rehearsal Best Be Used ?

❑ For **closed skills** use **internal** imagery.

❑ For **open skills** use **external** imagery.

❑ For **beginners** use **external** imagery.

❑ For **strength** use **lots** of imagery sessions.

❑ Mental rehearsal works **best** with sports that require a **high level of thinking** and those that require **lots of repeated movements**.

How To Perform Mental Rehearsal

❑ **relax** the athlete
❑ identify the **skill**
❑ **external** or **internal**?
❑ identify **key points** of the skill
❑ devise a **mnemonic** to remember the key points
❑ imagine and **focus** on the **key points**
❑ imagine and **focus** on **key performance**
❑ imagine as **vividly** as possible
❑ make the athlete complete a **verbal report** on how it felt
❑ **practice**

GOAL SETTING

❑   The setting of **future performance targets**.
     For example , times, fitness levels, league position.

❑   Goals appear to be most effective when they are **specific**, **immediate** and **challenging**, but also **realistic** and **measurable**. It is therefore important to set **small achievable steps for success**.

❑   **Short term goals** can be set over the period of a day, or a week or so.

❑   **Long term goals** can be set for a period of a month, a year, four years.

Guidelines for goal setting

❑   Set goals on the **basis** of **past performance**.
❑   Everyone is **different** and has different needs.
❑   Put goals in **writing**.
❑   Goals should be **challenging** but **attainable**, **specific** and **measurable**.
❑   Goals should be **flexible** enough for **revision** and **change**.
❑   Goals should have **target dates**.
❑   All **performance factors** should be included.
❑   Goals should include **effort** as well as performance.
❑   Goals should be related to the **overall aim** of performance.

Appendix 1 - Psychology of Sport - Overhead Transparency Sheets

Individual Differences
Social Influences on Performance
Stress and its Management in Sport

INDIVIDUAL DIFFERENCES

- ## Personality

  - ❑ The sum total of an individual's characteristics which make them unique.

  - ❑ Characteristics such as being shy, tense, relaxed, sensitive, aggressive, outgoing.

- ## Attitude

  - ❑ A learned emotional and behavioural response to a stimulus or situation

- ## Aggression

  - ❑ A response having for its goal the injury of a human being

- ## Motivation

  - ❑ An internal factor that arouses and directs behaviour

  - ❑ The power or drive behind why we do something

SOCIAL INFLUENCES ON PERFORMANCE

• Social Learning

❑ The effects that people can have on behaviour and performance. According to social learning theory (S.L.T.) all behaviour is learned.

❑ The greatest amount of learning takes place at an early age through socialisation. Socialisation is the process by which society trains its children to behave like adults.

• Groups and Teams

❑ Groups have a collective identity, a shared sense of purpose, and structured patterns of communication

❑ A successful team has good cohesion

• Social Facilitation

❑ The consequences on behaviour which derive from the sheer presence of others

• Leadership

❑ The process of influencing individuals or groups towards set goals

STRESS AND ITS MANAGEMENT IN SPORT

- ## The Nature of Stress

  - ❑ A stimulus resulting in arousal or a response to a situation

  - ❑ Arousal would be the state of activation or excitement a person has in any situation.

  - ❑ Contributed to by anxiety, which would be a reaction to stress resulting in over arousal.

- ## The Management of Stress

  - ❑ Educational Techniques

  - ❑ Cognitive Techniques

  - ❑ Relaxation Techniques

  - ❑ Mental Rehearsal

  - ❑ Goal Setting

Appendix 2 - Attitude Towards Physical Activity Questionnaire

STUDENT ATTITUDE TO PHYSICAL ACTIVITY QUESTIONNAIRE

(after Biddle S.J. 1996)

Physical Activity in the context of this questionnaire means exercise :

❑   which is suitably **vigorous**

❑   for at least **20 minutes** per day within a **game** or individual **sporting activity**

❑   which causes **heart rate** to increase to at least **120 beats per minute** at some time during the activity

❑   or which causes you to be **out of breath** either during or immediately after the activity.

❑   There are no right or wrong answers to the questions : attempt the questionnaire quickly, then calculate your score :   **You have problems as a sportsperson if your score is less than 27 !**

1)   **If I take part in vigorous exercise at least 4 times per week for 6 weeks, this would be good for my health -**

1 - very unlikely   2 - unlikely   3 - perhaps   4 - yes   5 - very good

2)   **If I take part in moderate exercise every day for 1 month this would reduce tension :**

1 - very unlikely   2 - unlikely   3 - perhaps   4 - yes   5 - very much

3)   **If I take part in vigorous exercise regularly this would enable me to socialise with my friends**

1 - very unlikely   2 - unlikely   3 - perhaps   4 - yes   5 - very much

4)   **How many times in a week on average do you take part in moderate or vigorous exercise ?**

1 - zero   2 - once   3 - twice   4 - three times   5 - four or more

5)   **If I take part in vigorous exercise regularly this would be a good thing :**

1 - not likely   2 - disagree   3 - perhaps   4 - yes   5 - very much

6)   **Being healthy and fit is :**   1 - very bad   2 - bad   3 - OK   4 - good   5 - very good

7)   **Reducing tension and anger is :**   1 - very bad   2 - bad   3 - OK   4 - good   5 - very good

8)   **Being able to socialise with my friends during exercise is :**

1 - very bad   2 - bad   3 - OK   4 - good   5 - very good

9)   **I intend to take part in vigorous exercise regularly over the next 6 weeks :**

1 - not likely   2 - no   3 - perhaps   4 - yes   5 - very much

A2.1

Appendix 3 - Achievement Motivation Questionnaire

STUDENT ACHIEVEMENT MOTIVATION QUESTIONNAIRE
(after Lynn - see Carron A.V. 1980)

1) Are you happy to be friendly with someone who is   no   - 1
    careless and disorganised ?   yes   - 0

2) Are you happy if food is wasted at a meal ?   no   - 1
                                                             yes   - 0

3) Are you happy to work with someone who is friendly   no   - 1
    but incompetent rather than someone who is capable   yes   - 0
    but difficult to be with ?

4) Are you able to completely forget your work when   no   - 1
    on holiday ?   yes   - 0

5) Have you always worked hard to be the best at your sport ?   yes   - 1
                                                                no   - 0

6) Are you happy to be late for lectures or classes ?   yes   - 1
                                                             no   - 0

7) Do you enjoy taking too much alcohol ?   no   - 1
                                                             yes   - 0

8) Do you get angry if one of your friends is late for   yes   - 1
    an important activity ?   no   - 0

Add up the total score - a score of zero would indicate a very low achievement motivation.

Appendix 4 - Attribution Questionnaire
STUDENT ATTRIBUTION QUESTIONNAIRE

(after Weiner, see Carron A.V. 1980)

A) <u>**Imagine a winning experience in your sport - one that you can strongly link with success and a good feeling about your sport.**</u>

1) **How much do you feel that your OWN ABILITY was an important part of the success ?**
1 - not at all   2 - not much   3 - perhaps   4 - a little   5 - very much so

2) **How much do you feel that your OPPONENTS LACK OF ABILITY was an important part of the success ?**   1 - not at all   2 - not much   3 - perhaps   4 - a little   5 - very much so

3) **How much do you feel that your GOOD LUCK   was an important part of the success ?**
1 - not at all   2 - not much   3 - perhaps   4 - a little   5 - very much so

4) **How much do you feel that your OWN HIGH EFFORT was an important part of the success ?**
1 - not at all   2 - not much   3 - perhaps   4 - a little   5 - very much so

B) <u>**Imagine a losing or very poor experience in your sport - one that you can strongly link with failure and a bad feeling about your sport.**</u>

1) **How much do you feel that your OWN LACK OF ABILITY was an important part of the failure**
1 - not at all   2 - not much   3 - perhaps   4 - a little   5 - very much so

2) **How much do you feel that your OPPONENTS HIGH ABILITY was an important part of the failure ?**   1 - not at all   2 - not much   3 - perhaps   4 - a little   5 - very much so

3) **How much do you feel that your BAD LUCK   was an important part of the failure ?**
1 - not at all   2 - not much   3 - perhaps   4 - a little   5 - very much so

4) **How much do you feel that your OWN LACK OF EFFORT   was an important part of the failure ?**   1 - not at all   2 - not much   3 - perhaps   4 - a little   5 - very much so

❑   **Now enter your attribution scores for both success and failure in the score chart on the next page.**

❑   **It would be helpful to record ALL scores for your group on the chart**

❑   **Calculate the average score for the group for each of the attribution factors.**

A4.1

SCORE CHART FOR ATTRIBUTION QUESTIONNAIRE

		Locus of Causality	
		INTERNAL	EXTERNAL
Stability	STABLE	Ability	Task Difficulty
	UNSTABLE	Effort	Luck

Appendix 5 - The Leadership Scale for Sport (LSS)

STUDENT LEADERSHIP SCALE FOR SPORT (LSS)
(after Chelladurai)

Mark the score for each of the following statements according to HOW YOU FEEL about the issue - NOT what you think ought to be the case.

1)   **As a sportsperson, I prefer my coach to emphasise hard, vigorous training to improve my standard of performance :** (Training and Instruction Behaviour)

   1 - not at all   2 - not much   3 - hardly   4 - perhaps   5 - a little   6 - usually   7 - always

2)   **As a sportsperson, I prefer my coach to make all the decisions :**

   (Autocratic Behaviour)

   1 - not at all   2 - not much   3 - hardly   4 - perhaps   5 - a little   6 - usually   7 - always

3)   **As a sportsperson, I prefer my coach to allow the group a say in deciding team aims and goals, a say in which activities should be done, and a say in which tactics and strategies should be used :**   (Democratic Behaviour)

   1 - not at all   2 - not much   3 - hardly   4 - perhaps   5 - a little   6 - usually   7 - always

4)   **As a sportsperson, I prefer my coach to be concerned about individual sportspersons and their wishes and feelings, to enable a positive group atmosphere to develop :**   (Social Support Behaviour)

   1 - not at all   2 - not much   3 - hardly   4 - perhaps   5 - a little   6 - usually   7 - always

5)   **As a sportsperson, I prefer my coach to recognise good personal results using praise as reward :**   (Rewarding Behaviour)

   1 - not at all   2 - not much   3 - hardly   4 - perhaps   5 - a little   6 - usually   7 - always

Decide from the scores which leadership style you prefer most.

Appendix 6 - The Least Preferred Coworker Scale (LPC)

STUDENT LEAST PREFERED COWORKER SCALE (LPC)
(after Fiedler)

❏   Think about the PERSON YOU WOULD LEAST LIKE TO WORK WITH.

❏   Mark the score for each of the following attributes of the person according to HOW YOU FEEL about this person.

❏   Note that this person does not have to be an enemy or someone you don't get on with - but someone whose work habits you find great difficulty in cooperating with.

Pleasant	8	7	6	5	4	3	2	1	Unpleasant
Friendly	8	7	6	5	4	3	2	1	Unfriendly
Rejecting	1	2	3	4	5	6	7	8	Accepting
Helpful	8	7	6	5	4	3	2	1	Frustrating
Unenthusiastic	1	2	3	4	5	6	7	8	Enthusiastic
Tense	1	2	3	4	5	6	7	8	Relaxed
Distant	1	2	3	4	5	6	7	8	Close
Cold	1	2	3	4	5	6	7	8	Warm
Cooperative	8	7	6	5	4	3	2	1	Uncooperative
Supportive	8	7	6	5	4	3	2	1	Hostile
Boring	1	2	3	4	5	6	7	8	Interesting
Quarrelsome	1	2	3	4	5	6	7	8	Harmonious
Self Assured	8	7	6	5	4	3	2	1	Hesitant
Efficient	8	7	6	5	4	3	2	1	Inefficient
Gloomy	1	2	3	4	5	6	7	8	Cheerful
Open	8	7	6	5	4	3	2	1	Guarded

❏   Now add up the scores and divide by 16 to obtain your mean score.

❏   Total score = _____   Mean score = _____

❏   A mean of less than 4.5 implies that your LPC is a task oriented leader type.

❏   A mean of more than 4.5 implies that your LPC is a person oriented leader type.

Appendix 7 - The Sport Competitive Anxiety Test (SCAT)

STUDENT SPORT COMPETITIVE ANXIETY TEST (after Martens)

- ❑ Look below at the list of statements about how you might feel when facing a sporting competitive situation.

- ❑ You have to decide whether you HARDLY EVER, SOMETIMES or OFTEN experience the feelings mentioned.

- ❑ Don't spend too much time on each statement - respond honestly and quickly by ringing the chosen answer on the sheet.

- ❑ There is no right or wrong answer to each statement.

- ❑ Remember to choose the answer you USUALLY feel.

1) Individual sports are more exciting than team sports :	hardly ever	sometimes	often
2) Before I compete I get a nauseous feeling in my stomach :	hardly ever	sometimes	often
3) When I compete I am concerned about making mistakes :	hardly ever	sometimes	often
4) Setting a goal is important when competing :	hardly ever	sometimes	often
5) When I compete I am a poor loser :	hardly ever	sometimes	often
6) Before I compete I am nervous :	hardly ever	sometimes	often
7) Just before competing I notice that my heart rate increases :	hardly ever	sometimes	often
8) Before I compete I am uncomfortable :	hardly ever	sometimes	often
9) Before I compete I am uptight :	hardly ever	sometimes	often
10) I enjoy the social side of competitions :	hardly ever	sometimes	often
11) Before I compete I am relaxed and confident :	hardly ever	sometimes	often
12) Waiting to compete is the worst part of the sport :	hardly ever	sometimes	often
13) I most enjoy sports which don't require a lot of effort :	hardly ever	sometimes	often
14) Before I compete I am calm :	hardly ever	sometimes	often
15) Before I compete I worry about not performing well :	hardly ever	sometimes	often

- ❑ Scoring for questions 2, 3, 6, 7, 8, 9, 12, 15 is as follows : hardly ever - 1   sometimes - 2   often - 3

- ❑ Scoring for questions 11, 14, is as follows : hardly ever - 3   sometimes - 2   often - 1

- ❑ Questions 1, 4, 5, 10, 13, are not scored.

- ❑ Mark your scores on the sheet, add them up and draw a conclusion about your anxiety state when competing.

- ❑ SCAT score = _____ .

A7.1

Appendix 8 - The State Trait Anxiety Inventory (STAI)

STUDENT STATE TRAIT ANXIETY INVENTORY (after Speilberger)

- ❑   Look below at the list of statements about how you might describe yourself.
- ❑   You have to decide whether you ALMOST NEVER, SOMETIMES or OFTEN can apply the statement to you or your feelings about yourself.
- ❑   Don't spend too much time on each statement - respond honestly and quickly by ringing the chosen answer on the sheet.
- ❑   There is no right or wrong answer to each statement.
- ❑   Remember to choose the answer you USUALLY feel.

1) I am calm cool and collected :   almost never   sometimes   often

2) I tire easily :   almost never   sometimes   often

3) Other people always seem happier than I am :   almost never   sometimes   often

4) I often feel depressed when things don't go my way :   almost never   sometimes   often

5) I feel comfortable :   almost never   sometimes   often

6) I feel tense or angry about things that have happened
    recently :   almost never   sometimes   often

7) I feel secure :   almost never   sometimes   often

8) Small things which happen to me give me great concern :   almost never   sometimes   often

- ❑   Score questions 1, 5, 7 as follows :   almost never - 3   sometimes - 2   often - 1
- ❑   Score questions 2, 3, 4, 6, 8 as follows :   almost never - 1   sometimes - 2   often - 3

- ❑   My STAI score = _____ .
- ❑   Does this score indicate a high or low trait anxiety level in yourself ?

Sports Psychology - An A level Guide for Teachers and Students

INDEX

REFERENCES

ACEP - Bump *Sports Psychology Study Guide.* Human Kinetics, 1989

**Alderman R.B. *A Sociological/Psychological Assessment of Attitude toward Physical Activity in Champion Athletes.* Research Quarterly, 41, 1970

Biddle S. *European Perspectives on Exercise and Sport Psychology.* Human Kinetics, 1995

Biddle S. *Psychology of Physical education and Sport - A Practical Guide for Teachers.* FIT systems, 1996

Bull S. *Sport Psychology.* Crowood Press, 1991

Bull S. *The Mental Game Plan, Getting Psyched for Sport.* Sports Dynamics, 1996

Bull R. *Skill Acquisition - A Teacher's Guide and Answers to Physical Education and the Study of Sport.* Jan Roscoe Publications, 1996

* Bunker L.K. et al. *Sport Psychology.* Movement Publications, 1985

* Carron A.V. *Group Dynamics In Sport.* Spodym Publishers 1988

* Carron A.V. *Social Psychology of Sport.* Movement Publications, 1980

* Carron A.V. *Social Psychology Of Sport: An Experimental Approach.* Movement Publications, 1981

**Cattell R.E. and Eber H.W. *Handbook for the 16 P.F. Questionnaire.* IPAT - Champaign Illinois, 1964

** Chelladurai P. & Carron A.V. *Leadership.* Canadian Association for PE & Recreation, Ottowa 1978

Christina R.W. *Coaches' Guide to Teaching Sports Skills.* Human Kinetics, 1988

**Corbin C. *The Motivational Rating Scale.* Medicine and Science in Sport 9, 1978

Cox R.H. *Sports Psychology Concepts and Applications.* Mosby, 1994

* Cratty B.J. *Psychological Preparation and Athletic Performance.* Movement Publications, 1984

* Cratty B.J. *Social Psychology of Sport.* Movement Publications, 1980

Davies D. *Psychological Factors in Competitive Sport.* Falmer Press, 1989

Davis R.J. et al *Physical Education And The Study Of Sport.* Wolfe, 1991

**Eysenck H. *Manual for the Eysenck Personality Inventory.* Educational and Industrial Training Service, 1968

**Fiedler F. *A Theory of Leadership Effectiveness.* McGraw Hill, 1967

**Fisher A.C. *Psychology of Sport.* Merryfield, 1978

Gill D.L. *Psychological Dynamics of Sport.* Human Kinetics 1986

Honeybourne J. *Physical Education And Sport.* Stanley Thornes, 1996

**Kenyon G.S. *Six Scales for Assessing Attitude Towards Physical Activity.* Research Quarterly 39, 1968

* Klavora P. and Daniel J.V. *Coach, Athlete and Sport Psychologist.* Human Kinetics, 1979

* Knapp B *Skill In Sport* Routledge And Kegan Paul, 1977

**Likert R.A. *A Technique for the Measurement of Attitudes.* Archives of Psychology, 140, 1932

Magill R.A. *Motor Learning: Concepts And Applications.* Wm C Brown, 1989

Martens R. *Social Psychology And Physical Activity.* Murray, 1975

Martens R. *Competitive Anxiety in Sport.* Human Kinetics, 1990

**Martens R. *Sport Competitive Anxiety Test.* Human Kinetics, 1977

* Mosston M. and Ashworth S. *Teaching Physical Education.* Merrill, 1986

**Osgood C. *Semantic Differential Technique: A Sourcebook.* Jam, 1976

Queensland Dept of Education *Video 5 - Motor Skill Acquisition.* Boulton Hawker, 1988

Roberts G.C. *Learning Experiences in Sports Psychology*. Human Kinetics, 1986
Roberts G.C. *Motivation in Sport and Exercise Science*. Human Kinetics, 1992
Schmidt R.A. *Motor Learning And Performance* Human Kinetics, 1991
Schmidt R.A. *Instructor's guide to Motor Learning And Performance* Human Kinetics, 1991
Schmidt R.A. *Motor Control and Learning*. Human Kinetics, 1988
Sharp R. *Acquiring Skill in Sport*. Sport Dynamics, 1992
* Silva J.M. et al. *Psychological Foundations of Sport*. Human Kinetics, 1984
* Singer R.N. *the Learning Of Motor Skills*. Macmillan, 1982
**Speilberger C. *Stress and Anxiety*. Hemisphere, 1977
* Stallings L.M. *Motor Learning From Theory To Practice*. Mosby, 1982
**Thurston L.L. *Attitudes can be Measured*. American Journal of Sociology, 33, 1928
Video Education Australasia *VideoFit2 - The Learning of Skills - Analysing Physical Activity*. Boulton
          Hawker, 1996
Weinberg R.S. *Foundations of Sport and Exercise Psychology*. Human Kinetics, 1995
Willis J.D. *Exercise Psychology*. Human Kinetics, 1992

* denotes book out of print at January 1997 - the books however may be found in libraries.

** denotes academic reference, original articles may be found in University libraries.